A TOUCH OF GREATNESS

Editor, publisher and author, Russi M. Lala began his career as a journalist in 1948, at the age of nineteen. Shortly after this, he became an executive in a book publishing house. In 1959 he became the manager of the first Indian book publishing house in London and in 1964 he founded (with Rajmohan Gandhi) the newsweekly *Himmat*, which he edited for a decade.

He published his first book, *The Creation of Wealth: The Tata Story*, to critical and commercial acclaim in 1981. This was followed by *Encounters with the Eminent* (1981); *The Heartbeat of a Trust* (1984); *In Search of Leadership* (1986); *Beyond the Last Blue Mountain: A Life of J.R.D. Tata* (1992); *The Joy of Achievement: Conversations with J.R.D. Tata* (1995) and *Celebration of the Cells: Letters from a Cancer Survivor* (1999). He has also edited, with S.A. Sabavala, a book of J.R.D. Tata's speeches, *Keynote* (1986). R.M. Lala's books have been translated into other languages including Japanese.

He has been director of the Sir Dorabji Tata Trust since 1985, and is the co-founder of the Centre for Advancement of Philanthropy, and since 1993, its chairman.

Books by the same author:
Available from Penguin:
- Beyond the Last Blue Mountain: A Life of J.R.D. Tata (1992)
- The Joy of Achievement: Conversations with J.R.D. Tata (1995)
- Celebration of the Cells: Letters From a Cancer Survivor (1999)

Other books:
- The Creation of Wealth: The Tata Story (1981)
- Encounters with the Eminent (1981)
- The Heartbeat of a Trust (1984)
- In Search of Leadership (1986)
- Keynote (edited with S.A. Sabavala, 1986)

A Touch of Greatness

Encounters with the Eminent

R.M. LALA

PENGUIN BOOKS

PENGUIN BOOKS

Published by the Penguin Group

Penguin Books India Pvt Ltd, 11 Community Centre, Panchsheel Park, New Delhi 110 017, India

Penguin Group (USA) Inc., 375 Hudson Street, New York, New York 10014, USA

Penguin Group (Canada), 90 Eglinton Avenue East, Suite 700, Toronto, Ontario, M4P 2Y3, Canada (a division of Pearson Penguin Canada Inc.)

Penguin Books Ltd, 80 Strand, London WC2R 0RL, England

Penguin Ireland, 25 St Stephen's Green, Dublin 2, Ireland (a division of Penguin Books Ltd)

Penguin Group (Australia), 250 Camberwell Road, Camberwell, Victoria 3124, Australia (a division of Pearson Australia Group Pty Ltd)

Penguin Group (NZ), cnr Airborne and Rosedale Roads, Albany, Auckland 1310, New Zealand (a division of Pearson New Zealand Ltd)

Penguin Group (South Africa) (Pty) Ltd, 24 Sturdee Avenue, Rosebank, Johannesburg 2196, South Africa

Penguin Books Ltd, Registered Offices: 80 Strand, London WC2R 0RL, England

First published in Viking by Penguin Books India 2001
Published in Penguin Books 2002

Portions of the book originally appeared in R.M. Lala's *Encounters with the Eminent*, published by the IBH Publishing Company

Copyright © R.M. Lala 2001
Copyright for illustrations vests with the individual illustrators

All rights reserved

10 9 8 7 6 5 4 3

For sale in the Indian Subcontinent and Singapore only

Typeset in Sabon by Mantra Virtual Services, New Delhi
Printed at Presstechlitho Pvt. Ltd, New Delhi

This book is sold subject to the condition that it shall not, by way of trade or otherwise, be lent, resold, hired out, or otherwise circulated without the publisher's prior written consent in any form of binding or cover other than that in which it is published and without a similar condition including this condition being imposed on the subsequent purchaser and without limiting the rights under copyright reserved above, no part of this publication may be reproduced, stored in or introduced into a retrieval system, or transmitted in any form or by any means (electronic, mechanical, photocopying, recording or otherwise), without the prior written permission of both the copyright owner and the above-mentioned publisher of this book.

Dedicated to
My dear Father
who, when I was away from him, used to write:
'You do not miss me now but you will when I am no more.'
This dedication is to affirm that I do.

Contents

Preface	ix
Azim Premji	1
Dr Banoobai Coyaji	12
B.P. Chaliha	20
C. Rajagopalachari	27
C.N. Vakil	35
The Dalai Lama	43
Fr. Henry Heras	53
H.T. Parekh	62
Jayaprakash Narayan	73
J.B. Kripalani	82
J.R.D. Tata	89
K. Kamaraj	101
K.M. Munshi	107
Lal Bahadur Shastri	113
Minoo Masani	122
Morarji Desai	132
Mother Teresa	141
M.S. Subbulakshmi	153
M.S. Swaminathan	160
Nani Palkhivala	173
N.R. Narayana Murthy	185

Sam Manekshaw	193
Sucheta Kripalani	201
Vijay Merchant	209
Vinoba Bhave	218
Zakir Husain	226
Epilogue	233
Select Bibliography	239

Preface

If we perceive with an open mind, every human being has some good quality which we can emulate with benefit to ourselves. Over the past five decades, I have had the privilege of meeting or getting to know a number of distinguished men and women. In each, I have found a touch of greatness and this has led me to search for the secret of their distinction in the context of their lives and times.

The political personalities whom I've featured I've met in the course of my editorship of *Himmat* (1964-75), which covered some whom I cannot claim to have come close to. Others, I had the good fortune to know well. In writing about men like Rajaji and K.M. Munshi, I feel happy that I can repay the debt of gratitude I owe them for the affection they extended to me.

I have learnt something from each one of those who has featured in this book. Some quality in their lives, or a sentence or two which I have quoted from them, has returned over the years to enrich and heighten my own life or helped me at a crucial moment. It is this wealth which I would like to share with others. For example, when I urged Rajaji, then in his late eighties, with his years as Chief Minister of Madras and Governor-General of India behind him, to write his autobiography, he told me with modesty, 'When the saints of India have not written their lives, who am I to write mine?'

When M.S. Subbulakshmi's husband, Sadasivam, the most faithful of his disciples, urged him to write about his life, he gave the same reply, but added movingly, 'Sadasivam, our job is to do our duty and to go.' In that one sentence Rajaji summed up what he thought was a man's purpose in life.

When I met Vinoba Bhave at his ashram in Paunar, it was his weekly day of silence. So he wrote out his replies in Hindi on a slate. He scrawled, 'Purity comes from God.' Brief but profound.

So often when I hastily rush to judge people, Mother Teresa's words return to me, 'If you judge people, you have no time to love them.'

From J.R.D. Tata I learnt how greatness and humility can exist side by side and make an impact on others.

There are moments in a nation's life when greatness abounds in its leaders and something of that greatness rubs off on people who live in their shadow. India passed through such a phase during her independence struggle and for a while thereafter. It was in these few decades after India's freedom that I met some historical figures like Jayaprakash Narayan, Acharya Kripalani and Morarji Desai. Some of them lived well into the 1970s and even beyond. Blessed with long lives these giants enriched India. Read together, their lives are witness to an era. For those who have lived through that era, *A Touch of Greatness* may be a welcome refresher. For those who are younger, perhaps the lives of these unusual men may provide some inspiration.

In preference to cricketers of today, I have selected Vijay Merchant of yesteryear as a representative of a period when cricket was cricket. Till the early 1980s, Vijay Merchant's record of average Test runs stood next only to Don Bradman's. His sense of discipline can serve as a model for those who wish to master the game.

Others covered include economist Prof. C.N. Vakil, who trained a generation of top economists; soldier Field-Marshal Sam Manekshaw; jurist Nani Palkhivala; and a rare artiste, M.S. Subbulakshmi. Twenty years ago I covered these lives in my book *Encounters with the Eminent*. I have retained these profiles and updated the information in most cases.

In the last twenty years, many interesting personalities have come into my life. I was fortunate to meet, and get to know well, Dr M.S. Swaminathan, who has moved from the Green Revolution he kindled in India to the nutrition security he is committed to now. It was a privilege to spend three days with the Dalai Lama in the hill station of Panchgani in the beautiful surroundings of the MRA Centre. Looking back, I was privileged to be a pupil and a friend of one of the great historians of our time, Fr. Henry Heras. So I have included his sketch.

It was H.T. Parekh who shaped two of India's largest financial institutions—the ICICI and HDFC. We worked in the field of philanthropy and along with others were instrumental in starting the Centre for Advancement of Philanthropy. It was my association with philanthropy too which led to Azim Premji calling on me. My biography of J.R.D. brought me close to Narayana Murthy much before he became a well-known name. Both these leading lights of information technology are covered by me not so much because of the wealth or fame they have amassed but because they represent a new and refreshing face of Indian industry. When ostentatious living had become fashionable, these two men arrived on the scene with their disarming simplicity, integrity and sense of mission and purpose. They are role models for young industrialists.

I responded to them so positively because like J.R.D. Tata (they both won the J.R.D. Tata Corporate Leadership Award) they work primarily not for profit but for the joy of achievement. Both have a vibrant social conscience. Both have reached where they are through different routes. Premji was born of a merchant prince. Narayana Murthy was one of five children of a modestly paid teacher, all of whose children stood first in class.

Narayana Murthy, who still stays in a three-bedroom flat he started his career with, reminds me of J.R.D. Tata in his later years. The house J.R.D. occupied in his younger days was large and sprawling. While I was working on my biography of J.R.D., for years he always received me in a small room with two chairs and a sofa, two telephones, a bookshelf and a desk. I thought this was his study. I later realized that it was also his bedroom and what appeared to be the sofa was pulled out when he wanted to rest. I asked him, 'Sir, no one in your position would spend his time in a room as small as this.' 'Why do I need anything bigger?' he replied. 'It suffices me.' How often when I am tempted to acquire material things which I don't really need, these lines come back: 'It suffices me.'

These personalities demonstrate what one can live for—and what one can live by.

Inadequate as my portrayals may be, I hope readers will appreciate meeting the people profiled in this book, as I have appreciated meeting all of them in person.

Mumbai, February 2001   *R.M. Lala*

Azim Premji

Honesty is good for the company. It is good for the customer. It is good for the staff. It is just good business.

The office phone rang. 'I am Azim Premji. I am in Bombay for a couple of days. Can I see you?'

A friend had told me beforehand that Premji wanted to create a large trust, mainly for primary education, and that she had given him my name in this connection.

On the appointed day and time in January 2000, I told my secretary, Saby, to wait at the gate of Bombay House, the Tata headquarters, lest Premji had to line up with visitors and delivery peons for a pass. 'He is in his mid-fifties,' I told my secretary, 'a handsome man with white hair, a thin moustache, and he will be in a suit.'

No sign of Saby. Then a firm knock on the door by a Tata official. 'Mr Lala, Mr Azim Premji to see you.'

'Where is Saby?' I asked, somewhat agitated. He replied, 'Mr Premji was waiting in the queue downstairs, and while passing by, I recognized him.'

It is typical of the humility of Premji, one of the richest persons in the world (the rank varies from three to forty-three), that he lined up with others. He eluded Saby for he was not in a suit, not even in a tie, but in brown pants and a short-sleeved shirt, and with somewhat dishevelled hair!

Illustration by Gautam Roy

'I've been visiting four municipal schools this morning,' he said with obvious delight. It was so different from his usual work.

'Would you like tea?'

'Only cold water. I can drink tonnes of it.'

Premji was excited about his visit and related how bright the children in those schools were. His interface with them reinforced his conviction that education was the right field for him to invest in.

I asked Premji how he started his life. He was at Stanford University, he said, only six months away from graduation, when his father died on 11 August 1966 and he had to rush back to take charge of his business. In view of his achievements since, Stanford University has conferred on Premji a degree in electrical engineering. 'My father had left debts and we sold the family jewellery and assets to pay them off,' he said.

'I remember your father. He was a well-known social figure whose photo often appeared in the evening papers.'

'He was well-known,' Premji agreed. 'He was president of the Bombay Chamber of Commerce and other associations but he had neglected his business and he died young. At the first AGM of the shareholders after he died, I presided. We were in the vegetable oil business. We still are. A shareholder got up and said, "You better hand over the company to someone else. You don't know how to run it." I got up, told him, "Come back after five years and see." At that time, we owned only 35 per cent of the company. Over the years, I steadily kept buying our shares.' The turning point came in 1977, when IBM was closed down. Premji was the early bird who moved in. He started with hardware and services, then moved into software. He has never looked back since. 'We saw a trend,' he told a journalist. 'We got technology at a reasonable price from a US company. We realized right at the beginning that computer companies in India were not investing in after-sales services. That became a winning proposition.'

That afternoon we discussed the pressing need for providing means of livelihood and vocational training to people and talked about the question of rural employment. He spoke of the size of his proposed foundation and how he would present his shares which, he said modestly, should rise in value by at least 20 per cent every year.

Even wealthy, perceptive businessmen can go wrong. By the time I met him two months later in March 2000, Wipro shares had shot up by over 200 per cent (each share being worth Rs 9,600) and put him in the number three slot among the richest men in the world. Later, the price of Wipro shares came sharply down! Knowing Premji, I think he may have been somewhat relieved not to be in the media glare for too long! By end-January 2001, *Forbes* magazine's list of the richest men featured him on the forty-second slot, with $6.9 billion—still the richest Indian in the world.

He owns about 84 per cent of Wipro shares, the market capitalization of which at its peak was over Rs 2,00,000 crore. Premji's own share then of Rs 1,50,000 crore ($35 billion) made him number three with Bill Gates and another person ahead of him. In all fairness it should be noted that Premji's wealth is notional. The moment he starts selling his shares, their prices will plummet. Premji's eggs are mostly in one basket. 'Premji's wealth is inflated but not his ego,' writes Aroon Purie, editor-in-chief, *India Today*, introducing a cover story on the Wipro chairman.

Assuming for a moment he could sell or place all his holding in Wipro at its peaked price of March 2000, *India Today* calculated that he could buy the whole of Reliance, Hindustan Lever and Infosys. Alternatively, his company could clear the entire fiscal deficit of the Government of India.

And yet, staggering though his wealth is, he told me, 'I live a very simple life. So does my wife.' He travels economy class by plane, avoids five-star hotels and wears clothes made in India. His peer in Infosys, N.R. Narayana Murthy, says, 'Premji is very focused and forever willing to learn from others.' A sound assessment. Premji is a man with a purpose, which is to do his job better and better all the time.

When he got the J.R.D. Tata Corporate Award for Leadership, he spelt out his own concept of leadership:

1. *Vision*: Vision is like a lighthouse, showing the way and pointing out hazards. It must be slightly beyond reach, but must not be an impossible dream.
2. *Values*: If vision gives direction, values set boundaries. Values need leaders to be absolutely transparent in whatever they do.
3. *Energy*: The leader must work both hard and smart, long and intensely. It's the only way to keep on top of the demands.
4. *Confidence*: Self-confident leaders assume responsibility for their mistakes and share credit with their team members.
5. *Innovation*: Ideas have limited shelf-life. The leader must create a culture of continuous innovation.
6. *Team building*: The leader must attract the best minds and create a sense of ownership in them. Not just by stock options but through emotional engagement.

J.R.D. would have been pleased with his choice for the award. J.R.D. built star performers and created in his team 'a sense of ownership', as Azim does. 'Ownership,' says Azim, 'is not just offering stock options. It has more to do with emotional engagement and interaction with the organization ... Leadership has to be built on values which make success enduring and helps in building resilient organizations that can stand up to any crisis along the way.'

For all that he has built up in thirty-four years, he claims no credit. He gives it to his team. To understand Premji you have to comprehend that he knows how to foster leadership in others, to delegate work, and to let his team-mates consult him but grow on their own.

His point three, on energy, he demonstrates himself. Premji starts work at eight in the morning and goes on working till 8.30 at night. He speaks softly, wastes no energy and prefers to reply in one or two syllables.

His point five, on innovation that 'Ideas have a limited shelf-life,' is significant. No one man has the monopoly of it. 'Ideas come from people and thus people are even more central to the success or failure of organizations in the future,' he says.

All his 10,000 employees feel they are part of a team. Premji respects no hierarchy, and goes to any employee. He has a hands-on style of working and goes into details.

He holds an open forum every quarter to increase the level of participation. He says, 'Leadership will be determined by its ability to generate excitement and enthusiasm to surface ideas.' Premji invites ideas from his people rather than impose his own views on them. And so he brings out the best in them.

Today, 90 per cent of Premji's business is with

computers, but 10 per cent is still his original vegetable oil business. For eight to ten days of the year he still goes round the retailers to get a feel of the market. The word Wipro itself comes from Western India Vegetable Products.

Premji cannot afford to rest for a single day in the fast-changing computer industry. He invests heavily in training. A century ago, he says, Jamsetji Tata moved India from trading to industry. 'Now we are in the middle of another powerful shift, from manufacturing into the knowledge era.' The mission statement of Wipro states:

OUR PROMISE

> With utmost respect to Human Values,
> we promise to serve our Customer with Integrity,
> through a variety of Innovative,
> Value for Money Products and Services,
> By Applying Thought, day after day.

Our next meeting was in Premji's office in Bangalore on the tenth floor of Du Parc Trinity, in the heart of the city.

Premji's office room was modest in size, not a piece of paper on his bare wooden table. No frills or clock or calendar. No files. The only pencil I could notice was the one in his hand.

I learnt that the founder of Pakistan, M.A. Jinnah, was a friend of his father, Hasham Premji. Both were prominent figures of Bombay in the 1940s. Jinnah was keen that Hasham Premji should come to Pakistan and is reported to have offered him the finance ministership. Hasham Premji declined.

'Why did your father not go to Pakistan?' I asked.

'I don't know the history of it. I only know the fact.' Not surprising as Premji was only a year old at the time of Partition. He went on about his father, 'I think he was, as most of us are, a strong Indian nationalist. What is so fascinating about Pakistan? In retrospect, he made the right decision.'

'But there was a great fervour for Pakistan (I meant among the Muslims) at that time,' I said.

'So it was in our country also (for India's freedom),' Premji replied.

His father was a charming social figure. I inquired if his father had influenced him. Premji replied, 'Of course.' It is from him that Premji inherited his passion for integrity.

'Where were you educated before Stanford?' I asked.

'St. Mary's High School, Mazagaon, Bombay, and two years at St Xavier's College, Bombay, 1962-63, 1963-64.'

'What books do you normally read?' I asked.

'Management books and business magazines,' Premji replied. Magazines which have items that are important or of specific interest to him are marked for his attention. 'What were your interests as a young man?' I inquired.

'Outdoors. I liked sports, quite a lot of it—skating, cricket, long walks, table tennis.'

'And at Stanford?'

'Tennis.'

'Do you still play tennis?'

'No, I jog now—ten to fifteen minutes.'

He jogs up ten flights of steps to his office most days.

'Did any books influence you?'

He shook his head.

'Any people?' I asked.

'No, but whenever you meet people, you take what is best

from them.'

Premji, by taking the best from whomsoever he has met, has shaped himself. What stands out about him is his value system. 'Honesty? Yes,' he says and adds, 'Honesty is good for the company, it is good for the customer; it is good for your staff. It is just good business.'

He once told a journalist, 'I would go to every conceivable length to preserve integrity at Wipro. Once, it took us eighteen months just to get a dedicated power sub-station activated because we refused to bribe. The power was for use in our vanaspati plant, which is heavily dependent on power. Yet we ran the plant for twenty months on captive generation which cost us dearly.

'Wipro has a clear policy that for all reimbursements, one has to spend the money to claim them. An employee in our Mumbai office travelled in second class and claimed reimbursement for first class. We found out about it and fired him. He was a union leader and the entire Mumbai office was on strike for two and a half months. But we didn't take him back. There is no point talking of integrity and not doing it when it comes to the bite.'

For Premji, integrity is not negotiable. 'It is a black and white issue. We do not look for grey and there are many shades of grey.'

Premji likes to do his own thinking. Unlike some corporate chiefs who lap up the idea of US consultants that only 'corebusiness counts' and the rest can be disposed of, Premji continues in his business of soaps and cooking oil, shoes, baby-feed bottles and tube lamps. He also sells PCs!

A striking quality about him is his humility. When asked about it, he replies, 'One realizes one is not all that great. At the end of the day, you ask yourself how much is due to good luck and how much have you really earned (achieved).'

'Do you believe in God?'

'I believe in luck. I don't believe in God. But I don't disbelieve in him.'

When half his age, I was in the same position. I related to him my journey to a faith.* He listened intently. He may still find faith himself.

'You carry your responsibilities so lightly,' I observed. 'You always look so relaxed.'

'No, no, no. I am certainly not relaxed. If I give you the impression I am relaxed, it is not correct.'

'What are the things that concern you about your business, about your country?'

'What concerns me is a very strong desire to do better than I'm doing, because one should have the modesty to know you can be doing better than you are doing. And that is a tremendous inner competition which can be constructive or very destructive because you are always racing with yourself.'

'But you are already a success. What more do you want?' I asked.

'Sustaining such success,' replied Premji.

'So it is a constant catching up with ideas?' I said.

'Or expectations,' Premji chipped in.

'Do you feel burdened by the trust reposed in you by people?' I inquired.

'Of course, I do.' He nodded.

'And decision making?' I inquired, adding, 'J.R.D. told me that when a quick decision was needed, he could take it swiftly but if there was no pressure, he would take his time.'

'You have to be like that,' Premji agreed.

---

* Covered in the chapter 'Journey to a Faith' in *Celebration of the Cells*.

'Does your wealth weigh on you?' I asked him.

'Yes, very much,' he said. He folded his hands. 'Please don't write about that. I'm getting an undeserved share of publicity. I am selling newspapers for people.'

'It must be irritating,' I said.

'Tremendously irritating. I've lost all my privacy. I can't even go to a restaurant.'

He added, smiling, 'If I could colour my hair and remove my moustache, I would do that, but they'll still trace me. I have become a caricature.'

'I feel sorry for you. But fame has its own price.'

When asked if Premji was any different earlier, before he became famous, his human resources chief replied, 'He is the same old man. He still comes to my office for lunch every day ... sharing my chapati and giving me his dal.'

His wife, Yasmeen, oversees work in the Hasham Premji Foundation. His son, Rishad, is working with GE in America. The younger son, Tariq, after graduating from a Bangalore college, is now working for a dot com.

I inquired, 'What has been the driving force of your life?'

'I suppose the driving force changes from time to time. At this point of time, apart from being successful in my job, one wants to give back to society what one has received from it.'

True to his word, Premji is starting a substantial Trust for primary education from which many stand to gain.

Dr Banoobai Coyaji

People like me are not great people but we are all meant to leave the world just a little better than we find it.

Banoobai Coyaji is Pune's best-known lady—and perhaps the most loved.

She constantly works on fresh projects to benefit rural women, specially adolescent girls. It all began in the 1970s. Coyaji found rural people flooding hospitals in Pune for minor ailments. The government had a scheme of Primary Health Centres but as they were second-rate, few patients went there. She asked the chief minister of Maharashtra to give her one Primary Health Centre to run and allot her the same amount of funds which the government would spend on it. She insisted she would get her hospital doctors to run the centres more efficiently. She did.

With the Primary Health Centres running efficiently, about 75 to 80 per cent of the patients were cured of minor ailments. As many as 15 to 20 per cent of the more difficult cases got treated at the two rural hospitals which she had started, and only about 5 to 10 per cent of the really serious cases landed in her Pune hospital. The rural hospitals were used to train nurses who belonged to the countryside as they seldom migrated to cities.

Coyaji tells doctors who apply to the KEM Hospital that

Illustration by Gautam Roy

until they work for six months in villages, she would not give them a posting at her city hospital. It works. When she started work in 1946, the hospital had forty beds. Today, it has 550 beds. The KEM Hospital is for the poor. Run by a Trust, it resembles a government hospital with crowds milling around. Coyaji's reach extends to 300 villages and foreign agencies constantly urge her to expand her programme. They are ready to back her financially.

One day Coyaji got a phone call from a woman with a foreign accent. She said she was speaking from the Philippines and asked her if she would accept the Magsaysay Award. Coyaji thought a practical joker was playing a prank on her. Hesitantly, she said 'Yes'. An hour later, when she went to her room at the *Sakal* newspaper, where she is a director, the news editor charged in and said excitedly, 'Madam, madam, you have got the Magsaysay Award. It has just come on the telex.' Then she realized it was no joke.

The prestigious Magsaysay Award has been given more often to Indians than to other Asians. The Magsaysay Award for Public Service was given to Jayaprakash Narayan, M.S. Subbulakshmi, Manubhai Desai, Baba Amte and L.C. Jain. In 1993, the $50,000 award went to the diminutive dynamo, Coyaji. The citation certificate reads:

'Banoo Coyaji
1993 Ramon Magsaysay Award
for
Public Service
in recognition of her mobilizing the resources of a modern urban hospital to bring better health and brighter hopes to Maharashtra's rural women and their families.'

For six years Coyaji served on the Scientific Advisory Group (STAG) of WHO that looks after women's health. In the course of that and other occasions she has visited 120 countries. While on WHO assignments, she has seen the plight of women in lands other than her own. Each appeal to WHO has to be cleared for action by her and her colleagues in STAG.

Ever since I have met Coyaji I have been intrigued not only by her achievements but also by her energy. The latter is a gift of God to her. It is the secret of her achievements that I was keen to explore. When I came to the end of my search, I realized that her life is of one piece and her energy level is high at eighty because of her sense of purpose, hard work, incredible organizational power and, above all, on account of her positive thinking.

'There are negative thoughts and positive thoughts,' Coyaji says. 'Judgement is usually negative. So are anger and jealousy.' Whatever the provocation, I have seldom heard her speak critically of another person. So her energies are canalized in creative channels.

'You can have,' she remarks, 'all the wealth and the health in the world but unless you do something for another person, you can't be happy.'

'Do something for another person'—that is another secret of her boundless energy and considerable achievement.

Coyaji sets a scorching pace. An early riser, she wakes up at 5 a.m. The morning goes in preparing papers or speeches. She is often invited to address Indian and international conferences.

At 7.30 a.m. she hears news on the BBC, glances at an English and a Marathi paper and at 8.30 a.m. leaves for the hospital. She is by qualification a gynaecologist, and had been for over fifty years director of KEM, one of the largest hospitals in Pune.

She is an authority on rural health, population planning, and the reproductive health of women. Coyaji speaks to young and old people alike—to young people on achievement, and to old people on growing old gracefully.

When I met her one day, she was to inaugurate a programme on Total Quality Care at the KEM Hospital. Pune is an industrial city home to many competitive companies that strive for quality production. 'Why should we not have total and continuous Quality Care?' Coyaji asked.

I asked her how her meeting had gone. 'I was amazed. Everybody in the hospital at different levels was there, from consultants to ayahs,' she said.

'What did you tell them?' I asked.

'I told them that to give total quality care, each one needed to ask "How can I do more?" We need introspection. I said I had examined myself and realized that till the hospital had about 200 beds, I had visited each patient daily. Now the hospital has 550 beds, and I have no time. It takes a minute, but it means everything to the patient if you touch and ask how he or she is.'

From there, she drove 40 km to her rural project at Vadu—the work that gained her international recognition.

She came to our house at 6 p.m., having driven 40 km in the heat of the summer, and drove back 40 km. I hesitated to ask her to join me for an important personal engagement I was going to. I knew her presence would help.

'Oh, don't worry about me. I have inexhaustible energy. I am born a Virgo (7 September 1917). It is written a Virgo has a back of stainless steel. I am strong as a horse and I work like a donkey.' Coyaji was then seventy-eight.

Those who work like donkeys don't do the strategic

planning which Coyaji does. She carries a monthly chart that accompanies her everywhere and every appointment is entered there. The KEM Hospital Research Society which she heads has thirty-one projects running at the same time, ranging from nutrition of women, to income generation, to training in health and hygiene. The sponsors include the Ford Foundation; the Population Council of the US; the Wellcome Trust, UK; and the J.R.D. & Thelma J. Tata Trust. Meticulous reports are given to each sponsor.

Along with all this, Coyaji has not only got a distinguished scientific advisory committee led by Prof. V. Ramalingaswami, but has also taken the trouble to recruit committed scientists and clinicians.

Coyaji's main focus is to improve 'the physical quality of the life index' and this includes life expectancy, infant mortality and adult literacy. For more than twenty-six years her projects have aimed at safe motherhood, maternal nutrition, integrated health care services and reproductive health. She moves with the times, and some of her projects undertake leadership training to empower women—who hold one-third of the panchayat seats—to increase their contribution for the betterment of their area.

The girl-child, Coyaji says, is treated terribly in India. Government schemes cover the girl-child from 0-6 years (Integrated Child Development Scheme) and also have a maternal child health scheme operation which focuses on the pregnant girl; the snag is that in-between the girl is left to fend for herself. Women come to Coyaji with other problems also. So from health, she has moved to income generation and then to basic education on hygiene for rural women.

Having no regrets for the past and no anxiety for the future, Coyaji is free to concentrate on TODAY. She quotes:

'Yesterday is a cancelled cheque. Tomorrow is a promissory note. Today is hard cash—use it.'

Till almost eighty, she spent most afternoons taking an active interest in the operations of *Sakal*. At 4.30 she took off for her clinic for a couple of hours, saying 'I have to make a living, you know.' She draws no salary from the hospital. When she completed fifty years, donations were raised in her honour to make improvements in the hospital.

Few people know that Coyaji is a pioneer of family planning. She had launched a family planning programme in 1946 with Shakuntala Paranjpe. In 1951, J.R.D. Tata focused national attention on the subject. When his Family Planning Foundation of India started (now called the Population Foundation), he included Coyaji on the board. In 1996, she wrote to a Tata Trust, saying, 'The biggest mistake we made in Family Planning was to neglect the male and his problems.' She got a grant to start the Tata Centre for Reproductive Health.

I have known few people as well organized as Coyaji. She plans on a grand scale but can also bestow immense care on individuals who are in need. 'By training, I am a gynaecologist. But at heart, I am a general practitioner, a counsellor.' When a woman in Bombay, whose husband was ill, needed her moral support, she drove all the way from Pune to be with her, had lunch, and speeded back for a 6 p.m. appointment at Lonavla, reaching home at midnight. A drive of 384 km.

At the age of eighty, in early 1999, Coyaji fell down. A swelling appeared on her shoulder. Her son, a Harvard-trained gynaecologist, advised her to go to hospital and get an X-ray done. But the woman who headed a hospital for over fifty years defied her doctor, 'I will disappoint the children whom I promised to meet at their school.' She told her daughter-in-law, 'Jeroo, put my sari on for me,' and off she went to the school. After going round the school for half an hour, she felt dizzy, settled down on a chair and was rushed to hospital. For the first time in her life, she was hospitalized and then housebound. When I visited her, I inquired, 'What is God trying to teach you through all this?' Without a moment's hesitation, she replied, 'To find myself.'

A little more than a year later, Coyaji was back in circulation. She was her old self again, doing her work at the hospital and supervising the work in rural areas which earned for her the blessings of tens of thousands of women.

Coyaji has appropriate jokes for most occasions. Once when the conversation veered towards the subject of heaven, she quipped that the Pope and a lawyer died at the same time and went to heaven. The Pope was assigned a tiny cell like everybody else, but the lawyer was given a well-appointed large suite. Observing this disparity of treatment, the Pope told St. Peter that heavenly justice was not quite what he expected. St. Peter replied, 'We have the likes of you every day but this is the first lawyer we have ever had.'

Perhaps, up there, there are some special suites reserved for doctors who serve humanity.

B.P. Chaliha

If the North-East disintegrates, it will be lost to India.

For thirteen years Bimala Prasad Chaliha wielded power as chief minister of Assam. As one of the country's seniormost chief ministers, his voice was respected in Delhi and in the higher echelons of the Congress. He retained his grace and humility till the very end. What is more, he continued his personal quest of applying certain principles to his public life.

He felt responsible for the 12 million people spread across the plains, the hills and the forests of India's North-East, from West Bengal to Burma.

In Assam one meets diverse strains of the human race—the Dravidian, the Aryan, the Mongoloid and the Austro-Asiatic. One feels that providence has a rich plan for this area. It has the potential to be the bridge between India and South-East Asia. This varied assortment of people is a potential asset, but when Chaliha came to power in 1957, many tribes in the region were restless. They were searching for an identity.

In 1960, Chaliha had to face language riots staged by those who wanted Assamese as a state language. But when it was introduced, the people of the hilly areas—later to form the state of Meghalaya—reacted with a demand for a separate state of their own.

Illustration by Manjula Padmanabhan

Chaliha's term spanned the reorganization of the North-East. When he came to power, Assam was a much larger state than it is today. But to meet the aspiration of its varied people, Chaliha agreed to the creation of separate states like Mizoram and Meghalaya. Nagaland had been carved out earlier. 'We are going through an experience of parochialism—hundreds of tribes in the North-East want to assert their rights and we must understand their desires, but any reorganization of the area should not be piecemeal. We have to plan for the long term and foresee what will happen in the years ahead. When the Naga Hills were formed into a separate state, I said it would not solve the problem and it hasn't. It has been a stimulus to other difficult situations and, if we are not careful, Assam will be torn to pieces,' he warned.

Later, Chaliha defined his idea of integration to me: 'Integration does not mean moulding people into one pattern. It means mutual respect and understanding—a process of fusion.'

As Chaliha had an innate understanding and respect for others, he was trusted by the Naga underground leaders. When I met the 'Vice-President of the Naga Federal Government' and its then 'Home Minister' in the forest of Chedma, they said, 'We can respect Chaliha.' Along with Jayaprakash Narayan, Chaliha was part of the Naga Peace Mission.

Tall and dignified, Chaliha was a thoughtful man, keen to listen, slow to talk. He was born in 1912 in a tea planter's family in Sibasagar, not far from the Burma border. While studying for his Intermediate in Calcutta, he left his studies to join the freedom movement.

When he was arrested in 1932 and jailed for six months, Chaliha utilized the time to invent an automatic spinning wheel. Gandhiji encouraged him to take training in handicrafts. After another spell of two years in prison during the Quit India Movement, he became a member of the Assam Assembly and a parliamentary secretary in the Assam Cabinet. In 1952, he became the president of the Assam Congress and was elected to Parliament. In 1957, he was brought back into state politics to become the chief minister.

Chaliha took a great deal of interest in the tribal people. Against the advice of some of his colleagues, he tried to go the extra mile and satisfy the restlessness of the Mizo people. His plans misfired. He was hurt by his failure and by the remarks of other men who dared nothing and achieved nothing. When I first saw him, a senior administrator of Assam advised me not to raise the Mizo issue with him as he was very sensitive to it. But as I got to know him better in later months, I asked him about it. 'Sometimes when you try to do good it may look like failure but I am confident that no good work ever fails. Its fruits come, even if they come late,' he replied.

A Naga woman, Mrs Rano Shaiza, recalls Chaliha's courtesy when she met him at New Delhi airport in April 1968. She was flying back home. Chaliha was in the lounge. Tea was ordered and when the waiter was bringing it in, Chaliha took it and offered it to Mrs Shaiza himself. Then, before the flight, he went to the counter, purchased three bars of chocolates and gave them to Mrs Shaiza for her children. Later, Mrs Shaiza was the sole member of the Lok Sabha from Nagaland.

Chaliha came to power at a difficult time. He could have clung to the status quo and the North-East would have gone up in flames around him, but he was a sensitive man who saw the signs of the time. Mr Kakati, who was editor of the *Assam Tribune*, remarked that Chaliha was 'unafraid to experiment'. 'He is always searching out new ways. Sometimes people fail him, but he continues. He is slow in coming to a decision, but once he does, he has the courage to see it through.'

The Assam Chaliha left behind him was territorially smaller than the one he inherited in 1957. But it was a more secure state because of the new-found relationship between people from the plains and those from the hill area. In the creation of this trust, Chaliha played a significant role.

The Khasis and the Garos, who inhabited the hills along Shillong, the state capital, were agitating for a hill state of their own. Stanley Nichols-Roy was the secretary of the All Peoples' Hill Leaders Conference. Though Chaliha and Nichols-Roy were in the same Assam State Assembly, the two leaders, once friends, did not even greet each other in the corridors of the House. Then, Nichols-Roy attended a conference of Moral Re-Armament in Panchgani and while introspecting, decided to measure his life against absolute moral standards of honesty, purity, unselfishness and love. His bitterness against Chaliha came to his mind. He went home and apologized to Chaliha 'not for my political convictions', as he put it, 'but for my bitterness which I have realized'. That day a new bridge was built. Chaliha saw a new factor emerging in the North-East and was quick to grasp it. He held Moral Re-Armament primarily responsible for the new equation between himself and his political opponent. In 1970, he said, 'Moral Re-Armament has transformed the climate of Assam. This is a fact. I speak as an administrator.' Soon after this, Chaliha agreed to the granting of autonomy for the hill people and later, for a separate state of Meghalaya. At the state's inauguration, the Governor of Assam and Meghalaya, B.K. Nehru, said: 'Seldom have such vast constitutional changes taken place with so much goodwill on either side.'

There was an intrinsic humility in Chaliha and a refreshing honesty. In the last talk we had in January 1969, he remarked, 'In politics sometimes one knows what is right but what if one finds it difficult to do?'

In October 1969 when the Congress was splitting, Chaliha, as the seniormost chief minister, made one last attempt to keep the party intact. He attended the working committee sessions of both the opposing groups and called for an end to the 'unseemly quarrel'. If he failed, it was not for want of trying.

By this time Chaliha was a very sick man but he continued in office till a few months before his death. He should have resigned much earlier. He paid the price with his health and ultimately his life. When he died in 1970 of cardiac asthma, his wife and children were by his bedside, as was his sister, Dr Nirmala Chaliha.

The six-kilometre funeral route was thronged with people from all over Assam. They had gathered for a last glimpse of their beloved leader. At a condolence meeting for Chaliha, a Mizo whose ancestral home was burnt during the disturbances in the Mizo hills, then a part of Assam, rose to pay his tribute. 'We felt he cared for us. When many Mizos suffered during the insurrection, it was Mr Chaliha who arranged for the education of hundreds of uprooted Mizo students and he granted each one of them Rs 80 a month for studies.'

There was in him a gentleness and concern for others that is rare in men in public life. At the same time, he had the larger vision. He had the statesmanship which India's north-eastern states need today.

Chaliha had his share of successes and failures, but in a world of expediency, he was bold enough to act according to his moral insight. And in doing so, he made the name of Assam shine in the rest of India.

C. Rajagopalachari

Elections and their corruption, injustice and the power and tyranny of wealth and inefficiency of administration will make a hell of life as soon as freedom is given to us. Men will look regretfully back to the old regime of comparative justice, and efficient, peaceful, more or less honest administration. The only thing gained will be that as a race we will be saved from dishonour and subordination.

Rajaji wrote these prophetic words in his *Jail Diary* in 1922, when the freedom movement was just gathering momentum. When he died fifty years later on Christmas Day 1972, one of India's last vital links with her freedom struggle snapped. Rajaji's was a multifaceted personality. He distinguished himself as a lawyer, an author and a statesman. He fought a gallant battle until the last. As he struggled for life in a Madras hospital at ninety-four, there was a constant stream of visitors, among them the President. When Rajaji left these earthly shores, he took with him a part of our history—and of our hearts.

One of my first recollections of Rajaji was in September 1963 when I saw him at Egmore station in Madras. The platform was studded with people waiting for a train from Delhi. Rajaji had come to receive some of his relatives. He

Illustration by Manjula Padmanabhan

was then eighty-five. Long before that, he had been chief minister of Madras and the Governor-General of India. Alone, the stooped figure with a walking stick was making his way up the platform. As he moved forward slowly, word passed through the throng and people made way for him yards ahead. It was the respect of a people, proud that one like him lived and walked amongst them.

As I got to know Rajaji better, I realized that in his frail body was a will of steel and the heart of a lion. He was great because he feared no one but his Maker.

Few men of this century have plunged so deeply into the day-to-day issues of their country and of the world as did Rajaji. Whether on Vietnam or nuclear tests, on the language issue or the internal politics of Madras, Rajaji had an opinion and made it known. Till the very end, he wrote for his English weekly, *Swarajya*.

Behind this man of the moment were the resources of a lifetime of reading and culture, of a rare strength of character and integrity founded on eternal values. These values Rajaji held high throughout his life and they, in turn, upheld him. Involved in immediate issues, he brought to bear upon them the breadth and space of his wide knowledge and immense wisdom.

On one occasion when the police arrested Rajaji during the freedom struggle days and sent him to jail, he took with him five books—the Mahabharata, the Bible, *Robinson Crusoe*, the plays of Shakespeare, and the writings of Plato. Even in his mid-eighties, he could quote as movingly from the Bible as he could from the Koran or from the Gita. He translated the Ramayana and the Mahabharata into English, because these two books were a part of his being.

In the 1920s, during his first imprisonment, he wrote the

Jail Diary. He clearly foresaw the future in which Swaraj would come.

Rajaji's career is a study in true leadership. He was a highly successful criminal lawyer who perceived the greatness of Gandhiji when the latter was still in South Africa and raised money for his struggle. Rajaji gave up his lucrative career to participate in the freedom struggle. When Gandhiji wanted emphasis laid on khadi and spinning, Rajaji left the comforts of his home and settled down in a remote village that was a three-hour journey by bullock-cart from the nearest station. There he tried out his experiment of propagating khadi. His ashram supplied cotton and paid for the spun yarn. Two thousand people, mostly women, earned a livelihood from his venture. Old wells were cleaned up for fresh water. Rajaji moved from village to village, travelling in a bullock-cart, and spread the message of temperance.

Personal initiative followed propaganda. The instance of the cobbler, Veeran, who, when drunk, had beaten his wife, showed Rajaji's flair. Importuned by Veeran's wife, Rajaji sent for the man, who denied drunkenness. 'But you were drunk last night and hit your wife,' Rajaji insisted. 'No sir, it is not true,' repeated Veeran.

Acting on a brainwave, Rajaji placed in Veeran's hands a pair of chappals which the cobbler had made and dared him, 'Swear on these chappals that you are telling the truth.'

His defences broken, Veeran fell at Rajaji's feet, owned up and vowed never again to touch liquor. Nor did he, as long as he lived. Well before his death, Veeran was given charge of the ashram's footwear unit, for which Rajaji, fair at using the awl himself, often had helpful ideas.

His early experience held Rajaji in good stead for the future. Leadership to him was the pursuit of causes, not of chairs. He was as happy to be in office as out of it. And when out of it, he avidly pursued his writing of books and articles. As his biographer and grandson, Rajmohan Gandhi, put it so well, 'He had an ear for other tunes besides freedom.'

Earlier, in 1942, Rajaji resigned from the Congress Working Committee because he disagreed with his colleagues over the Cripps Mission during World War II. Twice during the war, there seemed to be the possibility of a rapprochement between the Congress and the Government for a united war effort. The rapprochement did not come about. A seer among statesmen, Rajaji foresaw as early as 1943 the break-up of India and he alone tried to avert it by working out with Jinnah a loose federation for the subcontinent. For his exertions he was attacked by some members of his own party. Specifically, he got the Madras Legislature Congress Party to pass a resolution urging the All India Congress Committee (AICC) to concede to the Muslim League's demand for the separation of 'certain areas'. Had his suggestion been accepted, Partition might have been avoided. His colleagues were furious. Ultimately, Rajaji had to leave the Congress. Just a few years later, he returned to the party. He steered calmly through these patches of unpopularity and events proved him right. When India was partitioned and freedom came, he became Governor of West Bengal, and soon after, the first Indian to be Governor-General of India when Lord Mountbatten left.

Remarkable in his discipline (he washed his own clothes till he was ninety), he was also quick in his dispatch of work. Rajaji enjoyed the simple things of life. He once came to our home for supper. When he savoured the *rasam*, he called for the south Indian cook who had prepared it and complimented him. It was the high point of the cook's life.

Rajaji loved children. To him, they were a source of joy and he objected to birth control because, he said, it robbed families of this joy. He loved good books and once told me what a beautiful edition of Burke a friend had got for him from Oxford. If a neatly-typed letter was posted to him, in his reply he would tell the writer to compliment the secretary who typed it! His powers of observation were acute, as were the powers of his intellect.

Rajaji was concerned about humanity as a whole and therefore crusaded for the banning of nuclear tests. He led a delegation from India to meet President Kennedy on this score. He not only scanned the world horizon, he was devoted to scores of individuals in this land and they, in turn, gave him their unstinted loyalty.

He was distressed at the way the country was going under Jawaharlal Nehru's leadership. That is what prompted him to start the Swatantra Party. To him, India was the home of Ashoka and Akbar, and he was intolerant of many who were 'ruling from the once imperial capital, Delhi'.

'Freedom,' he said, 'was gained in 1947, but we lost it within a few years to the permit–licence raj which was mistaken for a superior kind of freedom. We must fight to restore India to India. As far as I am concerned, this battle is a moral conflict, not a matter of mere politics. I consider that the subjugation of the human personality to state direction is a dangerous experiment.' It was twenty years after his death that the dismantling of the permit–licence raj was initiated by Dr Manmohan Singh.

One of the most moving interviews I had with him was soon after the conclusion of the Indo-Pak war in 1965. His outspokenness during the war was frowned upon by the authorities. The then chief minister of Madras had even threatened him with imprisonment for his views. But Rajaji was undeterred. He was at peace—his was the voice of a man who had spoken his mind fearlessly.

When I met him, he was seated in his little office in the gardens of Kalki. He quoted from his favourite author, Edmund Burke, that one can rob a man of any material possession but not of the freedom to express his mind, for that is his most precious possession.

After stepping down as Governor-General, he became minister without portfolio in the Union government, and later Union home minister. In his late seventies, he made a comeback to state politics (for a second term) as chief minister of Madras. But these offices which came to him were not the result of his efforts to seek them.

If one searches for the roots of Rajaji's strength, one comes to the conclusion that it lay in his faith in God and in his unblemished family life. He was devoted to his wife, Manga, and nursed her with tender care during her illness. She died when he was thirty-seven, leaving behind five children. It was normal for men of his time to remarry but he refused to, and put aside all interest in that subject. When he was in his eighties, at a reception in Punjab, the chairman of the meeting referred to the fact that Rajaji's strength of personality lay in his being a brahmachari. Perhaps he thought so too for though Rajaji said nothing in public, after the meeting, he turned to the chairman and remarked, 'You may have a point in that.'

Steeped in scriptures, Rajaji searched for a renewal of his faith as he went through life. Discussing God, he asked me, 'If God is all-attentive, why did He permit twenty years of misrule in India?' I chipped in, 'Could it be that we were inattentive, rather than God?' 'Yes, that is true,' he said, nodding in agreement.

Rajaji was quick at repartee and delighted in giving unexpected answers. When someone congratulated him on his eighty-first birthday, he replied, 'No need to congratulate me. You have only to start early enough.'

In 1939, in the Congress Working Committee meeting, Ram Manohar Lohia, a Marxist, strongly attacked the conservative stand of the Congress, saying, 'I don't care a tuppence for this.' Instantly, Rajaji shot back, 'Lohia, you should swear in Russian currency—not British!'

Rajaji had a profound sense of history and an amazing disregard for his own part in it. On two occasions I ventured to propose that he might write his memoirs for the sake of future historians. On both occasions, he dismissed the proposal firmly. 'Let them find out,' he chuckled. A year before he died, when he was ninety-three, Sadasivam requested him to at least jot down the important events of his life. Rajaji replied that even great sages had not done so; who was he beside them? 'Man must do his duty and disappear.' So saying he clasped Sadasivam's hand, drew him close and said, 'Sadasivam, after I pass away, none need remember me.' After Rajaji's death, Rajmohan Gandhi wrote his biography.

The gift of repartee remained with him till the end. During Rajaji's last illness, when a drip needle was inserted in his left hand, he was uncomfortable and frequently touched it with his other hand. When the doctor told him not to, he acquiesced, saying, 'You mean the right hand should not know what the left hand is doing?' Forty-eight hours before he died on 25 December 1972, when his condition was critical, the doctor lent forward and asked him how he felt. Rajaji replied, 'I am very happy.' These were his last words.

C.N. Vakil

I learnt the art of dealing with students not only in their academic work, but also in their personal lives and career.

Two generations of India's economists passed through Prof. Chandalal Nagindas Vakil's hands and in an active lifetime of almost sixty years, he affected the economic thinking of the nation. Dr V.K.R.V. Rao, Dr R.N. Hazari, Prof. M.L. Dantwala, Dr D.T. Lakdavala and Prof. P.R. Brahmananda, all names to reckon with in the world of Indian economics, were among his pupils. And he was their affectionate teacher.

On 1 August 1921, in a corner of the Royal Institute of Science, Prof. C.N. Vakil was given a table and chair by the registrar of Bombay University and asked to establish the country's first department of economics in a university. 'There was no precedent,' Prof. Vakil was to observe later. 'I had no one to tell me what I should do. I had to think and plan the work. The structure that I evolved there was accepted by my senior colleague, Prof. K.T. Shah, who joined in November 1921.' The foundation of postgraduate teaching and research in economics in India was thus laid by Vakil. It was to evolve later into a school of economics. The Delhi School of Economics was founded by Prof. V.K.R.V. Rao only in 1950.

Illustration by Manjula Padmanabhan

'I learnt the art of dealing with students not only in their academic work, but also in their personal lives and career,' said Vakil. He taught at a time when the minds of students were aflame with the struggle for freedom and he often had to persuade them to finish their studies. M.L. Dantwala was in jail with his thesis unfinished. Prof. Vakil ensured that the right books and instructions reached him in jail so that he could complete his thesis. Among Vakil's pupils was B.T. Ranadive, who became a leading light of the Communist Party. Again, when Ranadive went to prison, it was Vakil who got permission to visit him there and discussed the thesis in the presence of the jailor. He got Ranadive the facilities for research and the chapters Ranadive wrote there were vetted by the jailor lest some incendiary writing be smuggled out by the firebrand.

Getting students to complete their thesis was not the end. He recalled, 'Research was not understood, not even known in those days. Students who did successful research work and got research degrees had to be placed in suitable work. The best means of doing so was publication of the thesis. This was difficult as no publisher would undertake the work, as such publications had no market.

'Arrangements were made with Longmans, Green & Co. to publish theses recommended by me on a commission basis. The cost of production would be advanced by them to be recovered from the sale proceeds. If a book was not successful in the market and the publishers could not get back their advance, they had to be reimbursed. For this they wanted a guarantee—I was the guarantor, with very little money in my pocket. The authors became known and they got suitable jobs and were appreciated—some of them occupy high positions in life.

'The Research Department of the Reserve Bank of India recruited research-trained economists. In the early days, they gave preference to graduates from Cambridge and Oxford. When I found that a well-qualified Ph.D. from the school was rejected, I approached the Governor and informed him that I had to close my shop or factory of manufacturing research trained personnel, as he, the consumer, was on strike. He saw the point and the door was opened.'

After thirty-five years with Bombay University, Prof. Vakil laid down the reins of office and went to Calcutta as director of the UNESCO Research Centre and commissioned research studies on the socio-economic impact of industrialization on South-East Asia. After three years of this assignment, he returned to Bombay and pursued his writing with vigour and spoke at various forums, propounding his economic theories. In the evening of his life, when seventy years of age, he was appointed as vice-chancellor of the University of South Gujarat. He also started a department of rural studies where boys from villages could apply themselves for the benefit of their people. Till he was eighty-three, he was active. The day he died, he had dictated an article for *Commerce* magazine. And in his file was the draft of a letter to Nani Palkhivala about a friend I had introduced to him, called Dr J.N. Mukherjee. Vakil said in the draft letter that Mukherjee had propounded such views in his book, *Forward with Nature*, that if it were Vakil's choice, he would award Mukherjee the Nobel Prize for economics. A few days before he died, he also sent me the draft of this letter.

I mention this to show that Vakil was a builder of men. There is no shortage in this land of those aspiring to fame and of those who are equally dogged in fending off those who may pose a challenge to them. Vakil was different. He was a true leader, for through him a host of economists came on the Indian scene—some as tall as himself. And Vakil rejoiced. A fitting index of his exemplary professional life is the quality and work of his students, many of whom are in the World Bank, the International Monetary Fund, the Reserve Bank of India, and other noted institutions. What delighted Vakil the most was that he did not have to run an 'employment exchange' in his later years as various companies were happy to engage the services of his students.

It was at the London School of Economics that he met his mentor, Dr Edward Cannan, who was a crusader against inflation. The wartime British government had followed inflationary policies. To bring it to its senses, Cannan filed a lawsuit against the chancellor of the exchequer to prove that he was being robbed of the value of his money by the government! The case became a sensation.

Cannan's student, Vakil, had to deal at home with a foreign government and was wise enough to steer clear of law courts. But he did publish a book during World War II that created a stir and put the British government in a spot. The little book was called *The Falling Rupee*. There were rumours he would be arrested but his wife says he told her not to worry. 'I know how to write,' he said. In his book, Vakil stuck to his economic case, but another economist, J.C. Kumarappa, quoted extensively from Vakil and spiced the observation with his political comments. For his labours he was prosecuted and sentenced to be His Majesty's guest for two years.

Vakil was born in Rander, Gujarat, in 1896 and came to Bombay when he was five years old. His nostalgia for those days of horse-trams and gaslights would linger. 'The trams took a little longer (than buses) but you never felt tired and exhausted (with fumes) as you do today.' When a pair of horses were not sufficient to haul a tram up Sandhurst bridge, another pair was stationed to be hitched to it. For four horse-power, scores of people could travel sans oil, sans pollution!

'You know one could easily recognize a person from his dress; Parsis wore pants with their coats along with caps, while Hindus wore dhotis and turbans or topi.' The Chowpatty beach, he recalled, was almost monopolized by Parsis. 'People in those days were more straightforward and simple. Life was frugal, parental authority more strict. And people did not come out (of their houses) so much,' he said.

Prof. Vakil studied at Elphinstone School and Wilson College. He secured a First Class First in BA in 1916 and topped the list again in MA. He did M.Sc. from the London School of Economics.

He always equated economics with the social context because he was interested in people. 'Economics is a subject which touches the life of everyone and an understanding of the essentials of the subject is essential.' His crusade against inflation touched a high point in 1974. Jointly or singly, Prof. P.R. Brahmananda (who was devoted to him) and Prof. Vakil addressed over a hundred meetings to mobilize public opinion against the erosion of their earnings. Under Vakil's leadership, 140 economists from fifty universities submitted a plan of action to the Union government to curb inflation. As with his earlier book, *The Falling Rupee*, in this case too 'there was no public appreciation of the effort from the government,' said Vakil, 'but in both cases, the main ideas were quietly accepted by the government in the form of anti-inflationary ordinances'.

Vakil had considerable foresight. During the Partition

when Dr Rajendra Prasad stated that Pakistan would not be fiscally viable, Prof. Vakil disagreed with him and was proved right. Further, Vakil predicted that the conflict in the economic interests of Pakistan's two wings would lead to a separation. He made this prediction in his book, *Economic Consequences of Divided India*, published in 1949. Twenty-two years later, Vakil was proved right.

Behind his profound learning was a warm-hearted man. In 1966, I requested him to write at some speed on the Budget for *Himmat*. He did. For the next decade and more, each year he wrote on that event and many other subjects. He wrote, in all, thirty books and pamphlets. He was a man of discipline who went for regular walks on Marine Drive and rejoiced to have a companion on his exercise.

On his eighty-first birthday Vakil was given a felicitation dinner by distinguished citizens and his pupils. In his speech, he spoke of those to whom he owed most in life. One was Chandra Shankar Bhatt, known as the Gyan Yogi of Rander, with whom in the early years he had studied the Gita. The other person was Shastriji Pandurang Athavle, who survived him. Among the many defects in our educational system, he said, was the absence of 'teaching of moral and ethical values or religion, and the want of familiarity with our own civilization and culture. It was fortunate that I had opportunities to make good this gap'.

At home, Vakil participated fully in the activities of his family. When he married, he was almost twenty-three and his wife was fifteen years. They celebrated the diamond jubilee of their marriage in 1979. He was deeply concerned about her welfare. It was his responsibility to remind her to take her medicine, and later on in life, he once travelled with her from Kerala to Switzerland to affect a cure for a complaint she had.

It was a privilege to pay Vakil my respects at his funeral. He died full of years in 1979. The flower-bedecked body was taken down the stairs of his Marine Drive home and placed near the gate for awhile. Then as they lifted him for the last journey, my eyes fell on his wife. Her eyes brimming with tears, she stood with her hands folded in a namaste as she had a long last look at the companion she had lived with for so long and so happily.

The Dalai Lama

I want to be remembered just as a human being—perhaps a human being who laughed often.

Once every year His Holiness, the Dalai Lama, goes to Bodh Gaya in Bihar to lecture on the Buddhist doctrine. In the cold of the north Indian winter, 2,00,000 people hear him out in the open air with rapt attention for five hours a day, for two long weeks. After one such gruelling session, he flew to Pune from where he made his way in a cavalcade of cars up the Sahayadri hills of western India for his next engagement. Suddenly, the Dalai Lama asked his driver to halt. The sun had set, and in the gentle evening light, the Dalai Lama had espied a beautiful flower he had never seen before and wanted to know more about.

When the Dalai Lama arrived at the hill station of Panchgani, a hundred policemen were assigned to protect him. Up in the hills during January the mercury drops sharply. Of the two police officers posted on his veranda, one dropped off to sleep. At 4.30 a.m., the door opened. A kindly figure in a robe tapped the dozing policeman on the shoulder and asked, 'Would you like some tea?'

The man who takes such an interest in people and despite his hectic schedule makes room for the impulse to admire a flower, carries within him the pain and suffering of six

Illustration by Gautam Roy

million of his people. He estimates that a million of his people on 'the roof of the world' have been tortured, imprisoned or killed. Occasionally he lets out an anguished, 'What have they achieved by these killings?' But not a word of bitterness escapes his lips and nothing is further from his mind than revenge.

Like Mother Teresa, he is intensely preoccupied with the person he is speaking to. He bends his tall figure quietly and his searching eyes look right through you as his broad smile encourages you to relax.

About the Chinese communists he says, 'The older revolutionary people were very sincere, they were aiming for a good thing but there was too much hatred in them.' And so, he says, not only their people but the leaders themselves 'lost happiness'.

He thinks of the 'happiness' not only of his own people but also of the Chinese. There is a unique spaciousness to his thinking.

He yearns for the freedom of his people to practise their faith, to protect their identity, and to regain independence. But he wants them to be liberated from within as well as from without. 'All people want to fight evil men; we have to fight the evil in men,' he says.

A Tibetan official in his thirties, who came with His Holiness to the centre of Moral Re-Armament in Panchgani, said after a few days, 'I find it quite difficult to forgive, having lost three brothers, four uncles and a half-brother of my father, all executed by the Chinese under Mao. But in order to reach a final conclusion for the Tibetan situation, we may have to forgive a hundred times.'

Those of us who harbour petty grudges can only bow our heads in shame at such magnanimity.

The Dalai Lama is a man with a twin mission in life. His first concern is his own land and people; the second is to promote compassion and love in other lands and peoples so as to bring about peace and harmony in the world. A man is known by the word or phrase he uses most often. For the Dalai Lama the word is 'compassion'. It features in many of his speeches. The holy book of the Buddhists, the *Dhammapadda*, relates the story of a disciple who asked the Buddha: 'What is the right action?' The Buddha replied, 'Any action which originates when a mind has compassion.'

This remarkable man whom the Tibetans look upon as the God-King was born in north-eastern Tibet in the family of a well-to-do farmer. In 1933, two years before his birth, the previous, revered thirteenth Dalai Lama had died. The search for a successor was on. The Regent went to a sacred lake, Lhamoi Latso, quite some distance from Lhasa, where it is believed that visions of the future can be seen in the waters. The Regent saw a vision of three Tibetan letters indicating 'north-east', followed by a picture of a monastery with a roof of jade green and a house with turquoise shell-like tiles. Various search parties were sent out, briefed in the strictest confidence to look for those signs, to locate the reincarnation of the late Dalai Lama.

When a search party came to the village of Dokham, they found a house with turquoise tiles. The senior Lama inquired if the family living in the house had any children and was told that there was a boy who was two years old. The senior Lama disguised himself as a servant and, while his companions entered by the front door, he entered by the rear door.

The child played in the servants' quarters with the senior Lama, who wore a rosary belonging to the thirteenth Dalai Lama. The child was fascinated by the rosary and asked for it. The Lama tested him the following day by giving him two drums to play, an attractive drum with golden straps, and a very small drum which the previous Dalai Lama had used. The child chose the small drum. When shown two walking sticks, he grasped the one used by the previous Dalai Lama. The party felt that they had come to the end of their search. The child was finally enthroned in Lhasa as the fourteenth Dalai Lama.

Patola Palace is a city within itself. The young boy was virtually confined within its spacious precincts. The Dalai Lama says, 'There must have been something lacking from my childhood without the constant company of my mother and other children.' While other children his age played and laughed, he was surrounded by solemn monks. That is why it is all the more surprising that he laughs so often and so heartily.

Only much later was his mother permitted to join him. His father's visits to the Patola Palace were not too frequent. When he did call, he would first visit the stables as he was very fond of horses, and then he would present himself to his son.

From his early days the young Lama was given a gruelling schedule of studies. At thirteen he was introduced to metaphysics. He felt as if he had been 'hit on the head with a stone'. He relaxed by taking his toys apart and then putting them together again. Then it were toy cars and planes that came in for such treatment. When he was a little older, he once dismantled a watch and got it to work again.

His curiosity was insatiable and still is. He would spread his atlas on the floor to see what lay below the roof of the world where he lived. He tried to teach himself English.

He was barely fifteen in 1950 when the Chinese marched into Tibet, which they claimed was historically a part of their country, although ethnologically and linguistically they are two separate peoples. An uneasy relationship prevailed between the young Dalai Lama and Beijing. He was allowed to come to India at the request of Prime Minister Jawaharlal Nehru, for the 2,500th anniversary celebrations of the birth of Buddha. As he laid a wreath at the memorial where Mahatma Gandhi was cremated, the Dalai Lama says, he wondered what wise counsel the Mahatma would have given him.

The Tibetan resistance was growing. In March 1959, the local Chinese commander asked the Dalai Lama to come for dinner at his army camp but without his palace guards. The Tibetans got wind of it, and fearing for the Dalai Lama's safety, they turned up in thousands and surrounded the palace to protect him. Events came to a head when the Chinese fired two heavy mortar shells which splashed into a marsh outside the palace gate.

The Dalai Lama was not afraid for himself, but he feared for the safety of the 30,000 or so people outside the gate who were exposed to Chinese fire. He was advised to leave the palace, at the risk of his life. He removed his spectacles, changed from his monk's habit into a soldier's uniform, donned a fur coat, slung a rifle over his shoulder and went out, unchallenged, onto the dark road beyond the palace crowds. A small party accompanied him. While the Chinese frantically searched for them, he crossed safely into India on 31 March 1959.

When the Dalai Lama and his entourage arrived in NEFA, now Arunachal Pradesh, a wave of sympathy for him swept across India. He was given refuge in India. A hundred thousand Tibetans followed him over in the following months and years. He repeatedly expresses his gratitude for

India's hospitality, but many Indians are grateful that such a man should dwell among them.

When the Dalai Lama arrived, Nehru was uncomfortable as he was apprehensive of arousing China's ire at giving him asylum. But public opinion ensured that His Holiness was treated in a manner befitting his status. Nehru selected Dharmshala in the hills of north India as a suitable abode for the Dalai Lama and his entourage as the Tibetans were used to a cold climate.

Today, this hill resort in Himachal Pradesh is a mini-Tibet. Monks in red robes are a common sight as are fresh-faced Tibetan children going to school. And in a modest house atop a hillock dwells Tenzin Gyatso, the Dalai Lama.

Foreign aid and sympathy spurred the rapid rehabilitation of the Tibetans. The Dalai Lama improved his hold over English to communicate better with the world. He took a personal interest in the education of his people, and three decades later, news items in the Indian Press lauded how well the Tibetans had done for themselves in a foreign land.

A whole generation of Tibetans has grown up which has not seen Tibet. Some of the younger generation are hotheads and believe in a violent struggle. In spite of untold provocations, the Dalai Lama has managed to convince his people that violence is not the correct way. In any case, he says, 'Where are we to get the money and weapons from?'

Having spent forty years in India, the Dalai Lama empathizes with India whenever disturbances take place. At a time when Gandhiji's philosophy of Ahimsa—non-violence—is being accepted in other parts of the world, he regrets that Indians are abandoning it. For him, Ahimsa is not only the absence of physical violence, but also the absence of all anger and ill will.

Whenever violent events rock India, he is keen to help, because, he says, 'I have lived in India all these decades and consider myself an Indian.'

Tibet is not only a unique country but also a unique civilization. Since their invasion of Tibet in 1950, and specially during the Cultural Revolution, the Chinese have destroyed 7,000 monasteries. Only seventeen exist today. They are tourist sites. The Chinese have ravaged and tortured millions. There is an attempt to flood Tibet with Chinese families and already there are many areas where the Chinese outnumber the Tibetans.

What should be the reaction of the Dalai Lama to all this? He was chosen not only as the spiritual but also as the temporal ruler of his people. Though no longer the temporal head in Tibet, their material well-being is as much his concern as their spiritual fitness.

Negotiations with the Chinese started in the early 1980s, but the talks made little headway. The Dalai Lama has issued a five-point peace plan which proposes that: the whole of Tibet be transformed into a zone of peace and non-violence; the transfer of Chinese people to Tibet be stopped; human rights and democratic freedom be respected; production of nuclear weapons and dumping of nuclear waste in Tibet be halted; and negotiations for the future of Tibet be started in earnest. The Chinese Government has paid scant attention to the Dalai Lama's proposals.

His Holiness' diplomatic triumph has been in getting the European Parliament, and what is more, the US Congress, to support the cause of Tibetan autonomy. The US Congress spoke of Tibet as 'an occupied land', notwithstanding the lure of trade with China. America's conscience has spoken louder than the coffers of its businessmen and the caution of its administration.

'For more than thirty years I have tried to find some understanding with the Chinese government,' says His Holiness, 'and towards this end, I have tried to make the maximum possible concessions. But with no result. Now, our only hope is global pressure on the US and the Western nations.' In a major concession, he agreed to accept the suzerainty of China if Tibetans were left to manage their own internal affairs. When the Chinese did not accept this, he thought it proper to withdraw his offer.

The award of the Nobel Prize to the Dalai Lama in 1989 was only a stepping stone to this international support.

In December 1990, I saw the Dalai Lama again, soon after the fall of the Berlin Wall, and loosening of the communist hold on East Europe and Soviet Union. I inquired how his delegation's talks with the Chinese were progressing.

'They talk, talk, a lot. But they don't listen,' he replied and laughed. I asked, 'Could you or anyone have expected these developments in the Soviet Union and East Europe five years ago or even a year ago?'

His Holiness came closer as if to catch my words better. I said, 'Within five years Teng and his hardliners may pass on, and Tibet may be liberated like Europe is being today.'

The laughing Lama became intensely serious. His eyes had a thin film over them as if he was asking himself, 'Can it really be so? Will it be so?' It was a moving moment. My heart reached out to him.

Within a few months of our meeting, East Europe was liberated and a confident Dalai Lama was predicting that the younger Chinese leadership would come and Tibet would be free.

Inspired by Mahatma Gandhi who fought for India's freedom but did not accept any office after independence, the Dalai Lama has decided to step down once Tibet is liberated. 'I will hand over all my powers to a new interim Government,' he says.

The Draft Constitution of Tibet, approved by him, envisages the abolition of the post of the Dalai Lama. And till that happens, he continues with his mission of educating the world about Tibet's cause. He also cares enough about humanity to teach us the virtues of compassion which we all badly need. Given his interest in people, it is natural that he wants each person to find his destiny. He is not only the Dalai Lama of the Tibetans, he is the Lama of the world. But if you ask him, 'Will there be another Dalai Lama?' he lifts his eyebrows and says, 'Does that matter?'

When asked how he would like to be remembered, he replies, 'Just as a human being—perhaps as a human being who laughed often.'

Fr. Henry Heras

The history of India is not the history of a nation, it is the history of a continent in which many peoples have been fused together; it is the history of many migrations, all of which have left gold dust in their trail; it is the history of many dynasties which all together have raised monuments which at times are real skyscrapers; it is the history of much knowledge contained in its profound sastras of world fame; it is the history of incomparable aesthetic conceptions at all levels of aesthetics; it is the history of very ancient literatures, the Dravidian and Sanskritic, which conceal inexhaustible riches of historical data and an imposing farrago of epic works, puranic and dramatic. Finally, it is the history of a constant desire to seek truth through the centuries, a desire that impelled the sages to withdraw into the forests, that invited kings to renounce their thrones, that dictated to the philosophers such metaphysical ideas as are not to be found in the most renowned civilizations of the ancient world.

I was sixteen years old when I went to a lecture by Fr. Heras on 'The Cradle of Civilization' at St. Xavier's College, Bombay. At this lecture, he traced the movement of the Indus Valley Civilization from Sumer to Egypt on the basis of an

Illustration by Gautam Roy

etching on the handle of a dagger. There was the seal of a boat and he compared it with what was found in sites in the Indus Valley Civilization as well as in Egypt, in the land of the Pharaohs. This single lecture decided my choice of subject in BA (Honours). I took Ancient India.

Many teach history. Some write books on history. But only an elite few can start a school of historical research. Fr. Heras did just that. He was born in a noble family which had a castle in Barcelona called Las Heras. In his teens he joined the church. At thirty-five, he had earned recognition as a writer of biographies and for a major work on the Jesuits in Chinese history. One day he was informed he was transferred to St. Xavier's College, Bombay.

'I did not know much of the history of India then. A few days after my arrival, Fr. Blatter, then principal of St. Xavier's College, asked me, "What history do you want to teach?" Without hesitation, I replied, "Indian history only." I still remember the surprise revealed in his face, "What Indian history do you know?" he inquired. "None," was my emphatic reply. His feeling of surprise deepened. "How are you going to teach it?" he finally queried. "I shall study," I replied. I began my study then, and I have not yet finished,' Fr. Heras said.

His distinguished student, Fr. John Correa Afonso, said, 'India for him was not a subject of study; it was an object of love. His love for India and her people was love at first sight.'

For Fr. Heras, the study of history was an extension of the search for truth. He used to quote the axiom of Cicero, 'It is the first law of history to dare say nothing which is false, nor fear to utter anything that is true in order that there may be no suspicion either of partiality or hostility in the writer.'

Fr. Heras penned a booklet, *The Writing of History*. His

first major work was *The Aravid Dynasty of Vijaynagar*. He soon realized that the field of history that needed to be explored was vast; as a result he founded the Indian Historical Research Institute. 'I required collaborators in my work,' he said. He built it up, he joked, with two lacks—lack of space and lack of money. At the institute, he 'introduced over a wide field new methods and vigour in the conduct of historical research, combining all the Western techniques of scholarship and an unusual capacity to understand and interpret Eastern philosophies,' said the *Times of India* in its obituary.*

The research institute drew 300 of the best scholars from India in his lifetime and eighty-six received their Ph.D.

Though I was immersed in journalism and was attempting to study law, I tried to do a Ph.D. under him. The subject was the movement of the Mohenjodaro civilization from the Indus Valley to Iran, a civilization which Fr. Heras believed extended right up to Ireland. I thought that because he was fond of me, he would make life easier for me. So on the first day of my Ph.D. work, I asked him, 'What should I read?'

He replied, 'Everything.'

Everything!

There were no short cuts with Fr. Heras. He had a sense of urgency about his work; at the same time, he had a great sense of peace. He also had a sense of humour which helped him to face adverse situations in life. I remember once he had asked a distinguished Western authority on history to a tea party and invited the vice-chancellor and others to meet the visitor. Next day, I inquired how the party went. He replied,

---

* 15 December 1956.

'He was to come at 5.30 p.m. It was 6.00, 6.30, 7.00 p.m. He never turned up.'

'But you must be very *angry*, father!' I exclaimed.

'No, I wasn't.'

'What did you do?' I inquired.

'Nothing. I just ate the cakes!'

'His lifelong scholarship never made him self-important,' observed his friend, Dr Bhabha, vice-chairman and managing trustee of the Sir Dorabji Tata Trust.

I remember an instance when I took a young man to meet Fr. Heras. In those days there were about six or seven young men who always hung around the main gate, where stood the impressive *patawala* (peon) with a red sash and a shining brass medallion on which was inscribed 'St. Xavier's College, Bombay'. These youngsters were usually present at the gate from 9.45 a.m. to 10.15, and again from 12.45 p.m., to watch young girls coming to college and going home. In-between, they spent their time in the canteen! If they had ever attended Fr. Estrellar's lectures on 'Truth, Goodness and Beauty', they had only absorbed the last of the three. One of them was Dicky Rutnagar, who is now a famous cricket commentator in England. When Dicky found that I knew Fr. Heras well, he said, 'Can you give me an intro?' I said, 'Sure.' So I took him to Fr. Heras's room. The latter was poring over his papers with his thick glasses. When we went up to his desk, he looked up, removed his reading glasses, and changed to his long-distance glasses. As I introduced Dicky, Fr. Heras eyed him up and down, then asked me firmly in his Spanish accent, 'Is he a student of this college?'

I said, 'Yes, father, you must have seen him at the gate.'

'Yes,' Fr. Heras replied, 'I have. But I thought he was aspiring for the post of a peon!'

In 1948, I recall Fr. Heras sitting at our home in Bandra on a sofa and my mother telling him, 'Can't you do something for my son? Can't you give him faith in God? Whenever I take him to a Fire Temple, what does he do? He starts reading an English book.'

Father chuckled and I was relieved that he, who could have been the 'hound of heaven', was not chasing me. In 1951, when I was in Europe and he in Spain, he insisted that I visit him there 'or don't face me again'. So, although I was short of money, I went all the way from England to Spain. He took me to Barcelona and to Monteserrat. In his own quiet way, he was proud of Spain. Though we had plenty of time together, never did he raise questions about faith and God.

In 1953, through my association with Moral Re-Armament, I did find faith in God and told him about it. He was moved and said, 'You know, son, when your mother told me about giving you faith in God, I used to pray to my guardian angel to pray for your guardian angel that you find faith.'

Unknown to me, he cared enough to pray for me.

The man who bestowed such affection and care on his students was engaged in major archaeological explorations with his students during holidays and created a small, but one of the finest museums of India's historical relics at St. Xavier's College. He was engaged in ceaseless research. The last twenty years of his life he devoted to studying the Indus Valley civilization and deciphering its script. Sir John Marshal, who discovered Mohenjodaro (meaning City of the Dead), held that it was an Aryan civilization. Fr. Heras said it was Dravidian in origin. He was sad and frustrated when those who were authorities in the field of history in Britain did not accept his findings. I asked him why that was so. And he indicated it was their pride and belief that they knew best.

The controversy about the origin of the Indus Valley civilization still persists. All I know is that from the study of the seals of Mohenjodaro he could decipher them and read them fluently, like 'Minas (fish) . . .'

He published his first volume of studies in *Proto-Indo-Mediterranean Culture* and told me proudly that the King of Sweden had ordered a copy. His second volume was written but the third volume was only in the form of notes.

In 1954, he received wide recognition on the occasion of the silver jubilee of the Indian Historical Research Institute. Soon after, he was struck down with illness. In his later years, what he loved most was a break at Kodaikanal, 'the most beautiful place in the world' as he called it. I used to occasionally send him chocolates from a company called 'Sprung' which he liked.

Two months before he died, he wrote four letters to me from Kodaikanal—three of them he called 'Epistles'. I would like to quote excerpts from some of his letters,

> You want to know what I am doing. I am doing what I have never done in my life, i.e. nothing. Contemplating the beautiful scenery from the infirmary room of this marvellous college (Sacred Heart), saying a late mass, whenever I can, nourishing myself with light food and meditating on Christ. He has sent me this illness in order to make me more like unto Himself . . . isn't that a cause of great joy for me to suffer for Him in order that I should enjoy with Him afterwards. There is no question of going for walks, ten or twelve steps are for me good enough to be terribly exhausted. But little by little I hope

I shall recover my old strength and then go for walks and shall be in need of Sprung chocolates . . .

I find much kindness here, much more than I ever deserve . . . All agree that my heart is very sound, my blood pressure excellent, head absolutely clear, but my nervous system and my stomach do not work well. This has produced a long period of under-nourishment which is the cause of this terrible exhaustion.

I later learnt he had cancer of the liver.

And, finally, in his letter of 26 October 1955, less than two months before he died, he wrote, 'Being ourselves created to God's image and likeness, the more we are similar to Him, the nearer we shall be to God. Try to do that yourself in your ordinary life, just as I am trying to do it here in suffering and pain.'

I met him next on 10 December when Fr. Balaguer, principal of St. Xavier's College, rang to say that Fr. Heras was very ill at St. Elizabeth's Nursing Home. I went to see him, and for the first time, I found him restless and unhappy. He said that a good part of his research was still in the form of notes.

As I had mentioned earlier, Volume I of his *Studies in Proto-Indo-Mediterranean Culture* had been published; he had written a good part of the Volume II, but the Volume III was only in the form of notes. He felt that after he died, no one would be able to unravel from his notes the secrets he had discovered. Though an infant in faith compared to him, I ventured to suggest that he surrender his work to God.

'But I have done all for the sake of the Virgin Mary,' he replied.

When I saw Fr. Heras two days later, a miracle had

occurred. He lay there with his right palm firmly planted on a large silver coloured crucifix. He seemed totally at peace. I knew then that he had surrendered everything to God and, in that recognition, found a measure of peace myself.

The following day, I got a phone call from Fr. Balaguer to say that Fr. Heras was no more. And I knew that he was prepared to meet his Master.

H.T. Parekh

Financial corporations should become the springboard for the country's further development in new areas of social progress.

On Tuesday, 8 November 1994, when I arrived in office from Pune I found there was a phone call from Hasmukhbhai Parekh. In his faint voice he asked, 'Will you come and have lunch with me today?' Having just arrived, I would have excused myself with any other person, but Hasmukhbhai had told me how lonely he was at home in his illness. So I went.

He was more subdued and quieter that day than ever before. For a man who had spent his lifetime in busy financial circles to be confined at home with just a nurse and a servant was a punishment. During his illness, I once asked him, 'What is your ailment?'

He replied, 'Loneliness.' Once he had a companion—his wife—and when she died, he published in Gujarati letters to her, recalling their life together. These letters were compiled in two volumes. It helped assuage the pain in his heart. His niece, Harsha, who worked as a librarian at the S.N.D.T., lived in the house and cared for him. She recalls, 'As children, we remember both of them as if they were one personality, complementary, dependent on each other.' When she died in 1970, he was fifty-nine. 'To be happy in marriage,' he used to

Illustration by Gautam Roy

say, 'it is not enough to be in love. One must also learn to accommodate each other.'

Conscious at lunch that this may be the last chance to meet him, I ventured to ask, 'Hasmukhbhai, how did you acquire your value system, your integrity?'

I thought he would say his faith in God or the impact of reading. He replied in two words, 'My mother.' He briefly added, 'We were six brothers and two sisters.' He did not say more, and as he had a respiratory problem, I did not press him to elaborate. The food at lunch was simple but as a concession to me, he had thoughtfully ordered some rosogullas.

His nephew, Deepak Parekh, who succeeded him as chairman of the HDFC, dropped in faithfully from his office, and so did friends from 5 to 7 p.m., but the rest of the day seemed to drag on endlessly for him.

Sixty years earlier, Hasmukhbhai was living in a chawl with his father, Thakurdas, who had a modest job in the Central Bank of India. Hasmukhbhai rose by sheer dint of his own efforts to shape two of India's largest and most respected financial institutions—ICICI and HDFC.

'Banking being my family background, I imbibed the spirit of bazaar banking from my father, but what shaped me more was the deep influence of my mother and the stamp of her self-effacing character. My generation also grew under the shadow of Gandhiji and his values and philosophy made a deep impact on me, though, I must confess, unlike my friends, I made practically no contribution to our struggle for freedom.'

His contribution was to come later.

After graduation from Wilson College, Parekh appeared for the coveted ICS exam in India. He failed. He then decided he would pursue higher studies at the London School of Economics. The family could not afford it. Somehow, he managed to raise the money for the first year, hoping to make his way to the second. In the UK, he twice appeared for the ICS examination but did not make it. After the first time he failed in England, he was too scared to tell his father. So he wrote to his elder brother, Shantilal, 'to break the news gently' to his father. Thereafter, he managed to take up a part-time job, study and pass out from the London School of Economics.

On his return, he could have easily got a government job. However, he chose a different path and joined a well-known firm of stockbrokers, Harkisondas Laxmidas.

At a felicitation function in his honour when he was seventy-five, he recalled, 'Twenty years in that unfathomable world of ups and downs, of booms and busts, of investment, speculation and gambling, of rumours and gullibility where people make and lose fortunes daily, taught me a lot, particularly because I was interested in the firm's various investment services such as gilt-edge, industry problems, balance sheet analysis, investment advisory role to institutions and individuals, and tackling problems of industrial sickness. My interests have always remained on the side of saving and investment which is now better known as merchant banking or investment banking, as against the more glamourous and popular activity of quick money-making through day-to-day trading in differences in the forward market.

'I also made use of these early twenty years in studying and writing on different aspects of the economy and economic policy, on money and banking and participating in public discussions on business management and industry, as also in annual meetings of companies. I also worked as a lecturer at a well-known college* for three years which gave me some facility for public speaking.

'I took special care to see that I was not identified with any industrial business house, and kept a certain distance from them to retain my independent identity and character and my institutional interest.

'Having served in a private firm, my joining ICICI was a novel experience of having to deal with a financial development institution organized for special purposes. ICICI was one of the earliest institutions sponsored by the World Bank in cooperation with the Government of India and the US Government. My friend, William Diamond, a passionate development official of the World Bank and an authority on the subject, defined development finance institution as "profit making but service-oriented". This made a deep impression on me and it became my obsession to work towards such an ideal.

'Managing a development corporation with the right kind of public image, non-bureaucratic, friendly and helpful, is possible only with a suitable band of professional colleagues who share a positive desire to serve, attract and encourage new entrepreneurs and are ready and willing to take reasonable risks. ICICI grew impressively to gain acceptance of the Indian business community, recognition of government and even became a showpiece for the World Bank.

'ICICI developed not only its financing activity but went further to become a development-oriented institution interested in development in its wider sense. Thus, ICICI initiated and made liberal grants to the setting up of other

---

* St. Xavier's, Bombay.

agencies, particularly in education and training. It sponsored the Institute of Financial Management and Research in Madras because Madras also needed a management development institution comparable to those in Bombay and Calcutta which were set up with government sponsorship.

'I was able to shape ICICI to my concept of a development institution; financial corporations should use a part of their large accumulating annual retained profits for wider development of skills, institutions and purposes which deserve encouragement and help. They should become the springboard for the country's further development in new areas of social progress.'

For him, public institutions had broader public responsibilities than profit, important as it was. They had to be 'service-oriented'.

At sixty-eight, when most men think of retiring, as he was stepping down from ICICI loaded with honours, he started a new institution, Housing Development Finance Corporation (HDFC). I asked him once, what made him start HDFC. He replied, 'I thought of it when I was in England at the London School of Economics.'

'But that must be fifty years ago!' I exclaimed.

He agreed and added that while in England he had observed how people owned their houses (on mortgage), unlike in India, and he wanted people here to enjoy the same facility. For years he had harboured a dream, and at the pinnacle of his career in ICICI, he launched HDFC.

To launch HDFC, he went to meet Secretary of Finance Manmohan Singh (later finance minister). Singh recalls his zest and enthusiasm for the project. He added, 'It (HDFC) was an unknown adventure (the first of its kind for housing finance in India). No one knew if it would click. But he had obtained promises from abroad (for funds) and he was enthusiastic.'

They became good friends, Singh told me. As Governor of the Reserve Bank of India, Bombay, 'Whenever I had any doubts, I went to him. He was always so positive, always coming up with new ideas. He never stagnated.'

Bimal Jalan, who many years later also became Governor of the Reserve Bank of India, was with the World Bank in the 1960s. Parekh is reported to have told him, 'What are you, an Indian, working in the World Bank for? Come with me. I will give you a job.' Jalan was thinking of returning to India and Parekh opened the door for him. Jalan became chief economist of the ICICI at the young age of twenty-eight and worked there for two and a half years. He steadily rose in his career—but not salary-wise for he was getting a better pay package in the World Bank. Jalan says that he joked with Parekh, 'You are the one who introduced me to poverty.' He says that Parekh was 'one of the greatest persons I met'.

When I asked, 'What made him great?' Jalan replied, 'His great desire to move ahead, great humility, simplicity of behaviour and a sense of public purpose.'

He added, 'He was so supportive of me. If the system had ten more people like him, we could do things.'

Parekh had no children and closest to him was the family of his elder brother, Shantilal. When his wife died, Shantilal's son, Deepak Parekh, moved in to live with him. After three years, when he went abroad, Deepak's sister, Harsha, took over to look after him. Deepak says he did so because he knew that staying alone, his uncle's health would decline rapidly.

Years later, when Deepak joined HDFC, Parekh was happy. Deepak's children were like his grandchildren. He told Deepak's wife, Smita, that the children could spend the weekends with him. They did. And one day when Smita dropped in, she found the busy banker sitting in bed with a children's storybook, reading to Aditya and Siddharth, the two boys stretched out on either side of him absorbed in the story. He became so fond of them that a mere Sunday was too short for him and once he rang Smita, 'Do you think the boys could take Monday off from school. Then I too will take a day off!'

Behind this warm-hearted institution builder was also a great builder of men. How did he train them?

'He spotted talent and went after such people and allowed them to work. He never told them what to do, but he did caution us to be careful,' says Deepak.

World organizations and the Union Government supported HDFC on the strength of Parekh's idea, his reputation and integrity. Manmohan Singh was Secretary of Finance. After giving clearance to the venture, he did not give direct government support to it but advised some government financial institutions to support it.

'He instituted a sense of values amongst us, not by instruction, but by example. His management style was marked by large-heartedness and human considerations,' said S.S. Nadkarni, once chairman of Securities and Exchange Board of India (SEBI). He trained young people by inviting them to be present at discussions with distinguished captains of industry, thus giving them a sense of belonging.

He was a visionary. 'HTP stood for financing new entrepreneurs long before venture capital became a slogan,' said Nadkarni. Many years before SEBI was established, Parekh recommended such a watchdog body for the stock market. He also advocated a Common Asian Market.

Parekh was the first to float a private firm to explore India's oil potential in the shape of the Hindustan Oil Exploration Company. He was a towering figure in industrial banking. In the first twenty-five years of ICICI, he spent a sizeable chunk in laying its foundation on sound business lines. He was governed by values, not by profit, by care and not by cash.

In the last decade of his life, he gave most of his time and energy to philanthropic causes. It was through his interest in philanthropy that our paths crossed and for eight years we worked closely in the Centre for Advancement of Philanthropy (CAP) which was founded to help Trusts and NGOs primarily with problems concerning tax laws, dealings with the charity commissioner's office, and to enable new Trusts to be formed.

When Parekh felt the time had come for him to step down, he twice asked me to take over the chairmanship. I declined and said we needed him. He was not to be outdone so easily. One day at the meeting of the board of directors, he got the better of me. He announced he was stepping down and proposed my name. I felt sorry for my colleagues on the board, for none of them dared say 'No' to him!

The Bombay Community Public Trust was promoted by him in 1991 to serve the city he loved. 'We need a clean and green Bombay,' he said. He took the initiative to construct Bombay's first public toilet by a corporate house at Dadar, through the HDFC. This resulted in several companies starting the facility for the city. In the Bombay Community Public Trust, he supported the adoption of a municipal school and made it a model for the remaining 1,000 schools of its kind. The respect he was held in resulted in various financial institutions giving donations to this Community Trust at his request. Sometimes a word on the phone would fetch Rs 5 lakh or Rs 10 lakh. At times, even at his age and despite his ill-health, he would visit people for his cause.

The managing director of a well-known company once expressed his surprise at Parekh's simplicity. Parekh lived in a typical middle-class home. He believed in the simple pleasures of life, in friendship and in reading. Every morning he looked forward to a walk and a chat with his friends at Marine Drive. When younger, his friends and he used to go for long vigorous walks. But as age crept in, the walk was more of an excuse to talk. One day while on his morning walk he started the practice of giving breakfast to one beggar. The numbers soon grew to two, four, six, eight, ten—not all of them deserving. So he switched to tea every Monday for fifteen to twenty of them.

In his last years, at about 8 a.m., Parekh would perch himself with his friends on the parapet of a building. I used to tease him about the 'Hasmukh Parekh Corner' at Marine Drive. He was a kind man who was able to achieve all he did because he did not think of himself but of others.

Author of a book, *The Money Market*, in his younger days, till almost the end of his life he was remarkably well-read and kept fresh clippings on matters concerning philanthropy from magazines like the *Economist*, London. His house was well stocked with books not only on finance but on different subjects and countries. He was particularly fond of biographies and the life of Jean Monnet, father of the European Common Market, had a great effect on him.

A disciplined man, he avoided the limelight. He had his morning walk with friends, but avoided social life and preferred reading and writing in the evenings.

Economist M.C. Dantwala, who knew him longer than

any friend—sixty years—said about him,

> Parekh is a man of few and simple words, uttered in a subdued tone. The latter trait is significant. It shows that he is concerned with communicating his ideas and sharing his thoughts rather than impressing others with his erudition and style, a common failing of successful persons. The unhastened delivery gives us a feeling that he is just reading his thoughts before us.
> The softness of expression does not mean he has no definite or even strong views. I know he has views on many economic issues under public debate. But he does not believe that strong views must necessarily be expressed in strong words or loudly. Their strength lies in the thinker's intellectual integrity. Strong words vanish quickly, sound thoughts have a longer life.

When I saw him six days before he died, he was breathing through an oxygen tube. He smiled sweetly but said not a word. And as I left, I thought, 'Devout Hindus believe in thousands of rebirths but for Hasmukhbhai this may be his last visit.'

The soul of a man like him who made homes available to so many will surely find shelter in a far more beautiful place.

Jayaprakash Narayan

My interest is not in the capture of power but in the control of power by the people.

'My world lies in shambles around me. I shall not see it put together in my lifetime.' So begins J.P.'s *Prison Diary* on 21 July 1975. It took almost two years more before, on 21 March, when his compatriots by ensuring a change of government in the elections, put his world together again. The tragedy was that it took J.P.'s own colleagues in Government less than two years to shake and almost shatter J.P.'s world once more.

Just a month before the March 1977 results, when the election fever was at its height, I was ushered into his room, number 1918, at Jaslok Hospital, Bombay. Wrapped up to his neck in a white sheet lay J.P. I was shaken to see him after a lapse of some years. His skin which had once been a rich tan now appeared dark and was shrivelled like a withered leaf. Only the warmth and twinkle in his eyes and his charming smile reminded me of the J.P. I had always known.

As his kidneys barely functioned, J.P. had to undergo a seven-hour ordeal every Monday, Wednesday and Friday when he underwent dialysis. They were marked in his diary as D-day—D for Dialysis. On days when he was not taking this treatment, he flew to distant places, addressed public meetings, gave press conferences and returned for treatment

Illustration by Manjula Padmanabhan

the following morning.

Though it was election time, we exchanged a few words on his future plans. He was eager to go round the country after the elections and educate the masses so that democracy would be strengthened from the village level upwards. In a faint voice he said, 'This is very important.' But fate willed otherwise.

A year later he said, 'If I had not fallen ill immediately after the March 1977 parliamentary elections, the scenario might have been entirely different. The political situation was explosive at that time; there had been a massive release of the people's pent-up feelings; and they were determined not to lose the opportunity by default. It would not do to deny—I am not being immodest when I say this—that I could have helped canalize all this into what might have opened up a path eventually leading to the restructuring, mind you, basic restructuring, of society. That was not to be, for God had it ordained otherwise.' He did not always speak of God in that vein.

The public life of J.P. spans half a century's struggle. He was born on 11 October 1902 in Sitabdiara, a village on the border of Uttar Pradesh and Bihar. His father, Harsudayal, was a junior official in the canal department of the Bihar Government. J.P. was seventeen before he saw a tramcar. Three years later in 1922, he was sailing for the US where he studied natural sciences, economics and sociology at various universities including California, Iowa, Wisconsin and Ohio. For a living, he worked in farms, factories and even washed dishes in restaurants.

On his return to India in November 1929, he was invited to stay along with his wife, Prabhavati, at Nehru's ancestral home, Anand Bhavan. Till the end of his life, Nehru was addressed by J.P. as bhai. Nehru's wife, Kamala, used to confide in J.P.'s wife.

J.P. was a colourful figure of the freedom struggle. He stirred many hearts during the Quit India movement. Captured by the British, he scaled the walls of Hazaribagh prison in November 1942 by tying one dhoti to another, and escaped to fight underground. As the machinery of the British Raj tightened to trap him, excitement grew in the nation. J.P. became a legend.

Earlier, in 1934, J.P., along with some bright, young men, founded the Congress Socialist Party. He spent hours with Gandhiji, talking about ends and means, about Marxism and God. Gandhiji was in no hurry. 'One day this man will speak my language,' he said, and Gandhiji was right. Four years after the Mahatma's death, J.P. did.

A Hindu, he had given up his religion to embrace Marxism in the US in the 1920s. It was not till thirty years later, in 1952, that at the end of a three-week fast in Poona, he bade goodbye to Marxism.

'I came to reject the philosophy based on Marxism because it did not offer the answer to the question, "Why should man be good, or why should anyone be good?"' J.P. articulated his new-found philosophy in an article entitled 'Incentives to Goodness', in which he stated,

> Materialism of any sort robs man of the means to become truly human. In a material civilization man has no rational incentive to be good . . . I feel convinced, therefore, that man must come beyond the material to find the incentives to goodness . . . The task of social reconstruction cannot succeed under the inspiration of a materialist philosophy.

The faith he discovered was real and was reinforced from time to time. Many years later, while in prison during the Emergency (1975-77), he jotted down in his *Prison Diary*, 'Last night, while offering prayers to Goddess Bhagwati, I had asked for a way out of this darkness and I got it this morning' . . .

> After Prabha's departure, I had lost interest in life. Had I not developed a special aptitude for public work, I would have retired to the Himalayas. My heart wept within but outwardly I followed the routine of life. My health too was deteriorating. It was in this hour of dejection that something unexpected happened which lit my inner self. My health also started improving and I experienced a new energy and zeal.

After Independence, J.P. saw Congressmen scramble for office. He shrank from it. He never offered to stand for any election, though in the 1952 elections he helped in the campaign of his Socialist friends. Although aloof from direct involvement in elections, his stock was so high that in the early fifties the Press called him 'Nehru's rightful heir'. But by that time J.P.'s thinking had moved to other fields of endeavour. The ideas of Gandhiji and Vinoba Bhave had captured his thinking.

He saw in the Bhoodan movement, which urged the landlords to donate land to the landless, the first attempt in history to bring about a social revolution through love. In the years to come, J.P. became a familiar figure in towns and villages. The dust of India covered him as he appealed for land to be donated. And as he walked through the land he loved, he took up various causes—some lost ones and others that proved popular. For him, the struggle for freedom in Hungary or Bangladesh was as important as that in his own country. He emerged as a rare public figure for three reasons: First, he wanted nothing for himself. Second, though polite to all, he feared no man. Third, he cared for people and had the humility and patience to listen to them.

One day a strapping rustic from Madhya Pradesh walked in to see him in Patna and asked if he would guarantee the security of dacoits if they decided to surrender as a result of a 'change of heart'. He revealed himself to be Madho Singh, a dacoit who had a price of Rs 1,50,000 on his head. This encounter resulted in 443 dacoits laying down their arms at J.P.'s feet in 1972.

Shortly after the dacoits surrendered, J.P. was asked by his friend, Minoo Masani, whether Madho Singh should stand for Parliament. Masani said, 'It is not such a bad idea after all. He would be in good company.' J.P. promptly replied, 'He would probably *not* be in good company, because he is a reformed dacoit.'

One sensed a certain expansiveness about J.P. Like Tagore, the windows of his mind were open to winds that blew in from all quarters.

With all his activities, J.P. kept up his reading of poetry, drama and political affairs. Until his kidney ailment undermined his health, he made a distinguished figure. His broad chiselled jaw indicated his strong determination. He always spoke in slow, clear and measured tones, as befitted a good teacher.

J.P. was every inch a gentleman. Prabhubhai Sanghvi, who was a close colleague of J.P., recalls an occasion when he was invited for lunch to J.P.'s home in Patna. 'He asked me to take a seat by his side and ordered his servant to serve special dishes prepared for me. He had instructed his servant to prepare khichdi and kadhi as he knew that Gujaratis like those dishes at dinner. He (J.P.) was served non-vegetarian food as per doctor's instructions. But he asked our permission before eating the non-vegetarian food. Such was his respect for others even in ordinary matters. For him, democracy was not a political dogma but a way of life.'

J.R.D. Tata confirms this gift of gentleness in J.P. In his Preface to his book *Keynote*, J.R.D. says:

> Of all the politicians I have known, Jayaprakash Narayan was, in many ways, the least representative of the breed, but one for whom I developed an unbounded liking and admiration. I first heard about him when, during World War II, he had gone underground in or near Bombay and indulged in the delightful activity of toppling Tata Electric high-voltage transmission towers in order to interrupt power supply to Bombay. He and his men soon discovered that, sawing through the legs of a tower which stood in a straight line with others, merely made it sag without breaking the electrical connection, while a tower forming an angle with others, similarly attacked, obediently collapsed on its side. Jayaprakash was betrayed to the police by the Communist Party who, by then, had somersaulted from being violent opponents of the war effort when Russia joined Germany's attack on Poland and Western Europe into sturdy supporters when Hitler attacked Russia.

J.R.D. met J.P. some years later in connection with some labour problem at Jamshedpur and was impressed by his transparent sincerity and gentle reasonableness, unexpected in an ex-revolutionary activist. It was, in fact, this unreasonable reasonableness, which J.R.D. believed, prevented J.P. from being an effective political leader and playing the powerful part he could have played in Indian politics. J.R.D. felt J.P. 'was too honest and too prone to see the other side and to accept compromises and would never be a party to the political shenanigans into which Indian politics increasingly sank in spite of Jawaharlal's effort to keep the political arena clean. Jayaprakash died a sad and disillusioned man whose friendship and regard I felt privileged to have earned'.

J.P. was a man of simple habits but was finicky about details. His shirt and pyjamas had to be sparkling white and properly ironed. If he wore a sherwani, the colour of his cap would match that of his sherwani, and he would hold a matching stick in his hand. Even when he was ill and went for treatment to Seattle, US, his secretary, Abraham, used to rush every morning to hospital to shave him before the doctor arrived. Such was his penchant for neatness that in his study books would be neatly arranged and periodicals tidily kept in fixed places. J.P. was fond of flowers. He had a small terrace garden at his residence in Patna. A vase of flowers was always by his side.

In early 1974, J.P. was asked by students and concerned individuals in Bihar to lead a movement for change in society. J.P. wanted more than the removal of the old order. He wanted the remaking of our institutions, our practices and even our national character. In 'total revolution', he said, everything had to change. Man had to change first of all, which was the most difficult part of the task. He put forward specific proposals, for example, on electoral reforms.

After the 1977 electoral victory of the Janata Party, when

tributes were showered on him, he simply said, 'No leader in history, no matter how great, whether it was Lenin, Mao or Gandhi, made a revolution. Revolutions happen. All that the leader does is to give it direction and control it. Otherwise it dissipates itself and there is a reaction . . . All I can take credit for is that I did recognize that a revolutionary situation had arisen and something had to be done.'

At the height of the upheaval in Bihar, J.P. said, 'My interest is not in the capture of power but in the control of power by the people.' J.P. himself shunned power and yet wielded tremendous influence.

His last months were sad. He often broke down when he saw the men he put in power break up the Janata Party which he had forged. A disillusioned J.P. told a reporter in July 1978, 'I helped them to come to power, because I had hopes that they would yet write a new chapter of India's history. But today I have come to realize that this enormous task of nation building is not within their capability.' On J.P.'s kidney problem, his secretary, Sachidanand, wrote that what pained J.P. the most was 'negligence' when he was under arrest by Indira Gandhi during the Emergency.

In October 1979, his old socialist comrade, Achyut Patwardhan, arrived in Patna to see J.P. When Achyut asked how he was, J.P. told him, 'Lingering, waiting for death.' And within twelve hours after Achyut's return to Varanasi, J.P. died in the early hours of 8 October 1979.

J.P. had the vision to look beyond immediate problems to the pressing need to change India's institutions—and above all the character of man himself, 'the most difficult task' he called it. Those who take on this struggle will be the rightful heirs of J.P.

J.B. Kripalani

There is no greater courtesy in a man than to be non-violent.

Few of Mahatma Gandhi's associates would have claimed to have known him for a longer period than J.B. Kripalani. He met Gandhiji way back in 1915 at a party in Calcutta. 'I wanted to see this curious man, as I had heard of his achievements in South Africa,' Kripalani said. Gandhiji had yet to make his mark on India.

Sometime later, Gandhiji wired Kripalani that he would stop at Muzzafarpur en route to Champaran, Bihar. Kripalani was then professor of history at the Government College. Gandhiji later wrote of Kripalani, 'It was an extraordinary thing for a government servant in those days to harbour a man like me.' Kripalani said, 'The professor downstairs was so frightened on Gandhiji's arrival that he packed his bags and ran away.'

When Kripalani told his students about the guest he was expecting, they were keen to meet him. They insisted on coming to the station even though it was late at night and urged Kripalani to receive Gandhiji with an *aarti*. For this a coconut was required. The only coconuts available were on a nearby tree. 'So I climbed the coconut tree, and pulled down a

Illustration by Manjula Padmanabhan

couple of coconuts,' recalled Kripalani. Noting my amazed look, he added, 'I was pretty supple in those days!'

Gandhiji moved to Champaran to spearhead the peasants' agitation against the indigo planters. The name of Champaran and Gandhiji echoed throughout the land. The Collector ordered him to leave in twenty-four hours. 'I am not leaving,' was Gandhiji's prompt reply. India knew then that a new force had emerged on the national scene.

'Kripalani,' said Gandhiji in his autobiography, 'could not but cast his lot with us . . . He was my gatekeeper-in-chief. For the time being, he made it the aim of his life to save me from *darshan*-seekers (visitors). He warded off people by calling to his aid now his unfailing humour, now his non-violent threats. At nightfall, he would take up his occupation as a teacher and regale his companions with his studies and observations and quicken any timid visitor into bravery.'

'What was Gandhiji's impact on you?' I asked Kripalani.

'I had to change all my opinions, to reread history in the light of non-violence,' he replied.

Kripalani was one of ten children. His father was an executive officer of a subdivision in Sind. 'I had to revolt against everything,' said Kripalani. And his record of revolt was impressive. He quarrelled with the principal of Wilson College, Bombay, where he had studied. Later, he could not teach for long in any institution because of his political views. He felt at home in Fergusson College, Poona, which was founded by dedicated nationalists.

'At what age did you become politically conscious?' I asked him.

'In college, I loved to enjoy myself. It was the time of the plague in Bombay. I would inquire how many plague deaths had taken place the previous day so that we might have a college holiday! Then one day, I picked up a paper called *New India* edited by Bipin Chandra Pal. I read it. It convinced me that the presence of the British in India was a sin that had to be got rid of.'

His father, a government servant, would hear no such views from his son. Frequently, they clashed. Kripalani taught in some schools in Sind but, 'I wanted no wrangling with my father, so I took the post in faraway Bihar. Father was a Persian scholar and lived up to eighty-five.'

In 1918, Pandit Malaviya wrote to Gandhiji, asking for the services of a young man who would help him in setting up the Benares Hindu University. Gandhiji recommended Kripalani.

'In 1920, came the non-cooperation movement and I left the university, and twenty-five students left with me. We started an ashram for village work,' said Kripalani.

A year or two later, a school with nationalist ideals was started, so that young men who had left their studies midway in response to Gandhiji's call could complete their education. Kripalani was one of its founder-teachers. Among his pupils was a very short young man with large and eager eyes. His name was Lal Bahadur. On passing out of Kashi Vidyapeeth, Lal Bahadur earned the title of 'Shastri'. Forty years later, Shastri became prime minister, and his teacher, Kripalani, sat on the Opposition benches and flayed ministers of Shastri's Cabinet.

From those early days, what Kripalani was most proud of was the ashram he had established. The ashram helped villagers to manufacture and market homespun khadi and had a turnover of a few crores.

In 1923, Sardar Vallabhbhai Patel invited Kripalani to become the principal of Gujarat Vidyapeeth, a national college which the Sardar had set up. It was there that Kripalani became known as 'Acharya', the learned teacher. In 1928, he left teaching. The national movement gained momentum in the thirties and reached its crescendo in the forties. Throughout this period Kripalani was at the heart of the struggle and in the inner councils of Congress strategy. From 1934 to 1946, he was general secretary, and then president of the Indian National Congress.

During this tenure, he got to know the leaders of undivided India well. He made some interesting comments on his contemporaries. On Jinnah and Nehru, he said, 'In fact, there was a good deal of similarity between Nehru and Jinnah. For one thing, they were both, shall we say, self-centred?'

On Sardar Patel, he said, 'He did not like anybody disagreeing with him. If he was angry with me, he would begin his letters, "Dear Kripalani". Jawaharlal Nehru, on the other hand, although I opposed him till his last days, always wrote "My dear Jeewan". They were very different, but Vallabhbhai was realistic enough to know that Jawaharlal had the backing of the masses more than him.'

'What struck you most about Gandhiji?' I asked him once.

'His utter sincerity and intensity of purpose. His love of the poor, his indifference to public opinion when he knew a thing was right . . . and his capacity to stand alone for truth,' said Kripalani.

Kripalani, too, learned to stand alone.

After Independence, Kripalani resigned as Congress president because he felt that Prime Minister Nehru did not extend to that august office the respect it deserved. In 1951, disillusioned, he resigned from the Congress and started the

Kisan Mazdoor Praja Party, which later merged with the Socialist Party. For a quarter of a century, Kripalani fought against the Congress. I recall his frail, hawklike figure rise in Parliament and, pointing at the massive array of Congress benches, thunder at them, or wither them with his sarcasm. They heard him with respect.

Though over ninety years of age, he campaigned extensively during the 1977 elections against Indira Gandhi. When engaged in this exercise, he cracked his collarbone. Undeterred, he started again after a few days of rest. At the victory rally, Kripalani warned the people that politicians were men with feet of clay and should not be put on pedestals. His words were prophetic, for the feet of clay showed up pretty soon.

After the Janata victory in March 1977, it was left to Kripalani and Jayaprakash Narayan to meet Janata MPs and decide on who should be prime minister. Jayaprakash Narayan was inclined towards Jagjivan Ram. It was Kripalani who suggested it should be Morarji Desai. Kripalani revealed this to Minoo Masani who told me about it.

When Kripalani was in his forties, he married Sucheta, twenty years his junior. The marriage was initially opposed by Gandhiji and, though he later gave his permission, he declined to give his blessing, saying he could 'only pray' for them.

Forty years later, Kripalani wrote, 'Gandhiji's prayers were enough, and with his prayers we lived a happy life.' In 1974, Sucheta died. They were devoted to each other. Kripalani says he expected to die before her, but the Almighty willed otherwise. In his eighties, Acharya Kripalani wrote movingly, 'It is the ambition of every Hindu that at the moment of his death, he should remember his God. That has been my ambition throughout my life. But it may not be. I am afraid even at that supreme moment, her memory and her image would intervene. I pray that it may not be so and at the supreme moment I may remember my Maker.'

J.R.D. Tata

I do not take myself too seriously.

In the mid-1970s, a convoy of cars and buses sped along a highway in Sweden with motorcycle escorts on either side. A helicopter constantly hovered over it for the cargo was precious. In this convoy were men of finance and industry who between them controlled billions and who could be held up for vast ransoms. Every six months they met either in America or in Europe under the aegis of the Chase Manhattan Bank. Among them were Dr Giovanni Agnelli, president of Fiat; the president of Ford Motors; the biggest shipbuilder in the world, who was from Hong Kong; a member of the House of Mitsubishi; David Rockefeller, president of the Chase Manhattan; and Dr Henry Kissinger. The most carefree in this select company was J.R.D. Tata from India. He assured his friends, 'Nobody will kidnap me, for nobody will want a ransom in rupees!'

When not on one of his travels in India or abroad, he stayed with his wife in a bungalow that defiantly stood its ground when skyscrapers soared all around it. The sprawling bungalow, set amidst scores of shady trees, is a vestige of a bygone era of space and leisure. One room in that home was allocated for a workshop and a gymnasium which J.R.D. proudly showed to his visitors.

Illustration by Manjula Padmanabhan

J.R.D. preferred to spend a good deal of his time in what appeared to be his study. There was a whole shelf of books on aviation, another on military ventures and warfare, and one on sports cars and motor racing. He liked to read crime fiction, lighter books like David Niven's *Bring on the Horses*, and books by Louis L'Amour. J.R.D. was not just a collector of books but was an avid and enthusiastic reader. After one of my first interviews at his home, I returned with three of his favourite books including one by Alexander Woolcott, which J.R.D. was keen I should read.

For my interviews connected with his biography we used to meet in what I thought was his study. About three years later, I discovered that this room was not only his study, but also his bedroom! I ventured to say, 'Sir, nobody in your position will live in a room as small as this.'

He replied, 'Why? It suffices me.'

J.R.D. was an interesting product of two continents.

Born in Paris in 1904, J.R.D. schooled in Paris, Bombay and Yokohama. Most of his education was in France. In order to improve his English before going to Cambridge, he was sent to an English Grammar School.

According to J.R.D., his mother was a very resourceful, intelligent and adaptable lady who—with five children—single-handedly packed up her household items in France and came to India to be with her husband, who was in the House of Tatas. As she went back to her home country every year or two, J.R.D.'s education was regularly disrupted. His grandmother was a very formidable lady. 'Her husband was a humorist and after some time with her,' says J.R.D., 'the gentleman ran away as anyone would have, had he been married to my grandmother.' Perhaps J.R.D. inherited his sense of humour from his French grandfather.

Louis Bleriot, the first man to fly across the English Channel, had a house on the coast of France near the Tata's country home. Bleriot's pilot, who used to land a small plane on the beach, once gave J.R.D. a joyride. It was then that the fifteen-year-old boy decided that one day he too would fly. He had to wait ten years for it to happen.

After school, he was drafted for a year into the French army and assigned to a regiment in France called *Le Saphis*. At the end of his time there, he expected to go on to Cambridge where a place was reserved for him. But his father summoned him back to India to join the Tatas. It was to rankle with him for decades that he never went to a university. His father must have had a premonition, for he died nine months later and J.R.D. took his place as director of Tata Sons, which controls India's largest industrial group. J.R.D. was twenty-one.

Though he missed his college education, he undertook his own education after office hours, studying books on various aspects of business. When he was in his early twenties, while recovering from typhoid, he would come to his room at the Taj, throw himself in bed and study. When his sister Rodabeh pleaded, 'Why don't you rest Jeh, you are tired and unwell,' J.R.D. replied, 'I want to be worthy of Tatas.'

Flying was a passion with J.R.D. He was the first one to qualify within India to fly. He got his licence, which bore on it Number 1, on 10 February 1929. When I asked him what was the greatest adventure of his life, he replied, 'The flying experience. None can equal that.' He added, 'When you are on your own in that little plane at the control without an instructor, and the plane speeds on the runway and finally takes off—you know you are in the air on your own.'

In 1930, the Aga Khan Trophy was offered for the first

Indian to fly solo from India to England or vice versa. J.R.D. competed, taking off from Karachi to London. When he landed at Aboukir Bay in Egypt, he found that Aspy Engineer, the other contender, flying from London to Karachi, was stranded in the desert airfield for want of a spark plug! J.R.D. sportingly parted with his spare one and they continued their journey in opposite directions. Aspy beat him by a couple of hours. 'I am glad he won,' said J.R.D., 'because it helped him get into the Royal Indian Air Force.' Later, Aspy was to be the second Indian to be the chief of the Indian Air Force.

J.R.D. recalled that in 1932, 'One October morning as the sun rose on the eastern horizon, a single-engined Puss Moth plane took off from Karachi with a load of mail for Bombay. As the plane hummed and rose the pilot said a word of prayer.' And so India's first airline—the Tata Airlines— was inaugurated.

In 1948, J.R.D. went on to start Air-India International. Within ten years he was president of International Air Transport Association (IATA). Though the airline was nationalized in 1953, he remained at the helm of Air-India till 1978, making it one of the most efficient airlines in the world.

In 1938, at the age of thirty-four, he became the chairman of the largest industrial group in India, which he led with distinction for fifty-two years.

When I asked him why he was appointed at such a young age as chairman of Tata Sons, when senior, more distinguished men like Sir Homi Mody and Sir Ardeshir Dalal were on the board, he shrugged it off and said, 'It was an aberration.' When pressed for a reply, he said, 'Perhaps, because I was hard working.'

With his limitation of formal education, how did he

discharge his responsibilities? 'Because of a lack of technical knowledge, my main contribution in management was to encourage others.' He elaborated on how he dealt with each man in his own way and brought out the best in people. 'At times, it involved suppressing yourself. It is painful but necessary . . . To lead men, you have to lead them with affection.'

With more than sixty years of experience in top management, he developed his own philosophy and method where leadership was concerned. 'One of the qualities of leadership is to assess what is needed to get the best results for an enterprise. If that demands being a very active executive chairman, as I was in Air-India, I did that. On the other hand, in one of our other companies where I know that the managing director likes to be alone and will get the results that way, I argue with myself and decide that it will be stupid for me to come in the way when the other person has a capacity for focusing his genius and producing the results. Often a chairman's main responsibility is to inspire respect.' And then he added, 'Don't forget, I like people.'

It has been one of the richest experiences of my life to have known him as the chairman of the Trust I was director of and as his biographer.[*]

Every interview with him was an exhilarating experience. Each time I learnt something. I once mentioned to him, 'Of course, Sir, you believe in excellence.' He retorted sharply, 'Not excellence. Perfection. You aim for perfection, you will attain excellence. If you aim for excellence, you will go lower.'

---

[*] *Beyond the Last Blue Mountain—A Life of JR.D. Tata.*
The Joy of Achievement—Conversations with J.R.D. Tata

J.R.D.'s sympathies were wide. Unlike some of us, he never accepted the poverty around him. He wanted the best for India and her people. Though he headed a group of almost 100 companies, he could also care intensely for individuals.

In 1989, doctors diagnosed that I had cancer and they gave me some rigorous treatment. I did not want to burden him with my problems. But he came to know that I was suffering from a violent reaction to chemotherapy. One day when I went for one of my interviews, he told me he wanted to send me to the US for treatment. He did. He happened to be at Lexington Hotel in New York the same time as I was. A day before I met my doctor, he told me, 'I do hope they will stop your chemotherapy.' The following evening I rang up to tell him that the doctor had advised me to discontinue that treatment. He said, 'You don't know how happy you have made me today.' A few days later, my wife and I happened to be in the Lexington foyer when he left the hotel to fly elsewhere. My wife went up to him and said, 'Mr Tata, I want to thank you for all you have done for Russi.'

'Don't thank me, my dear,' he said. 'Thank his faith and his God.'

One of the most memorable evenings of my life was on the spacious grounds of NCPA. J.R.D. was being felicitated by Tata employees on the Bharat Ratna awarded to him in 1992. Towards the latter part of his speech, this patriarch, then eighty-seven, addressed his people, 'My friends, I should say my children . . .' Every eye was moist because they knew he meant it. Then the man who had done so much to give India economic strength went on to say, 'An American economist predicts that India will be an economic superpower in the next century. I don't want India to be an economic superpower. I want India to be a *happy* country'.

He had formed his own guiding principles of life which he spelt out:

> Nothing worthwhile is ever achieved without deep thought and hard work.
> One must think for oneself and never accept at their face value, slogans and catchphrases to which, unfortunately, our people are too easily susceptible.
> One must for ever strive for excellence, or even perfection, in any task however small, and never be satisfied with the second best.
> No success or achievement in material terms is worthwhile unless it serves the needs, or interests of the country and its people and is achieved by fair and honest means.
> Good human relations not only bring great personal rewards but are essential to the success of any enterprise.

In the 1960s and 1970s Tatas were not growing as fast as some other industrial groups were. All the major schemes J.R.D. put forward to the Government of India from 1960 onwards, including the manufacture of cars and the setting up of a suitable fertilizer complex in Mithapur, were stymied while other inductrial groups were given licences to grow. I observed to him in 1979, 'Could it not be said that the other industrial groups have grown faster than Tatas over the last years?'

J.R.D. replied with feeling as well as firmness, 'I have often thought of that. Had we resorted to some of the means that some other companies did, we would have been twice as big as we are today. But I would not have it any other way.'

J.R.D.'s strength was that he applied his beliefs in practice. Vasant Seth, founder of Great Eastern Shipping, while in college was once standing at a bus stop with three women colleagues. A limousine rolled up at the bus stop. The driver asked if anybody wanted a lift. The girls hesitated but Seth hustled them on the rear seat of the car while he perched himself next to the driver. To impress his lady friends he turned to them and said, 'Do you know whose car we are travelling in? We are travelling in the car of Mr J.R.D. Tata.' The distinguished man at the steering turned to him and said, 'Young man, this car does not belong to Mr J.R.D. Tata. This car belongs to the Tata Iron & Steel Company.'

J.R.D. was one of the most highly decorated Indians with many awards bestowed on him.[*]

Yet till the end of his long life, he regretted not being sent to college. Eight months before J.R.D. died, while driving to the airport, I asked him, 'Sir, you are genuinely modest and humble, but suppose you had been to Cambridge, would you have been as humble and modest as you are today?'

He thought for a moment and replied, 'I think I would have been even more humble because although I may have been a Doctor of Engineering from Cambridge, I would have known how little I knew of other subjects.'

Though very fond of children, he and his wife had none of their own. Even in his eighties, he worked till late in the

---

[*] The Padma Vibhushan, 1955; Knight Commander of the Order of St. Gregory the Great (a Papal Honour), 1964; Knight Commander's Cross of the Order of Merit of the Federal Republic of Germany, 1978; Commander of the Legion of Honour of the French Government, 1983; Gold Air Medal of the Federation Aeronautique Internationale, 1985; Bessemer Medal of the Institute of Metals, London, 1986; Edward Warner Award, International Civil Aviation Organization, 1986; Daniel Guggenheim Medal Award, 1988; The Bharat Ratna, 1992; United Nation's World Population Award, 1992.

office. When his secretaries would say, 'Sir, it is late. Would you not like to go home now?' J.R.D. would reply, 'What have I to go home to?' Neither children nor grandchildren were there to greet him on his return. There was his wife in the wheelchair with a nurse and a Dalmatian to receive him. In some ways he had everything, in other ways, nothing. He lacked some of the simple joys of life but it never dampened his spirits.

As years advanced, he was searching for a deeper faith in God.

I had my most moving interview with him two weeks before he left India forever for Geneva. He was discussing with me a hymn he liked, *Abide With Me.* 'God has to look after 800 million people in this country and 6 billion in the world, how can I expect him to look after me or abide with me?' I replied, 'It depends on your understanding of God. If God is your friend, you would.' Then I quoted the lines,

> He walks with me
> He talks with me
> He tells me I am his own.

'It is beautiful,' he said and then added, 'Walk with me! I think it is damn cheeky to say that. He has so much to do. Why should he bother about me?'

He said that he had prayed more in the last year, though he had prayed earlier when someone near him died, but never for himself.

This was in mid-September 1993.

On 4 November, J.R.D. was removed to the Geneva State Hospital with very high fever and a urinary infection which was brought under control.

He knew he was nearing the end and he wanted to go. He told a friend in French, *'Comme c'est doux de mourir.'* (How soft/gentle it is to die.)

On 26 November, two of his doctors, Dr Dalal and Dr Farokh Udwadia, both from Bombay, met him.

Dr Udwadia asked, 'What is your major complaint, Jeh?'

'Don't you know, my dear Farokh, it is age. After all, I am eighty-nine.'

J.R.D. had given up eating a couple of days earlier. 'Don't behave like a child,' remonstrated the doctor. 'You must eat.'

'Why do you want me to eat at my age? Why should I eat? Why should I not just shut my eyes and go?'

Later the same day, Simone Tata met J.R.D. in hospital. J.R.D. seemed somewhat brighter. Between spells of drowsiness and alertness, he suddenly opened his eyes and said in French to Simone Tata, 'I am about to discover a new world. (Pause.) It is going to be very interesting (pause), very interesting.'

'As he said it,' Simone Tata recalls, 'his eyes were sparkling as if he had seen a glimpse of that new world.' After that he went back to sleep.

Three days later, in the early hours of the morning, he passed away.

Many were the tributes he received from India and abroad, but perhaps the tribute that would have touched him the most came from his old company, Air-India. Their tribute to him was:

He touched the sky
and it smiled.

He stretched out his arms
and they encircled the globe.
His vision made giants out of
men and organizations.

K. Kamaraj

Regionalism is going up, nationalism is going down.

It was a simple village wedding in Salem district. There were only fifty guests. The chief minister's car rolled up and out stepped Kumaraswamy Kamaraj. The bride's father, an impoverished Congress worker, had invited the chief minister but least expected him to attend the marriage.

Kamaraj had a leisurely breakfast with his friend and they talked of old times. 'We were prisoners together once. We are still friends,' said Kamaraj. He took the coconut respectfully offered to him, entered his car, and drove on. A minute later, he asked the driver to stop his car. He pulled out his cheque book, wrote out a cheque and asked the driver to give it to his friend. The gesture and the sizeable sum made the Congress worker's eyes well up with tears.

Kamaraj's stature was the product neither of his high ideals nor his personality. It came from his remarkable touch with the people, and his unconcern for financial rewards. There was hardly a Congress worker in Tamil Nadu whom he did not know personally. And he never forgot a face.

The man who enthroned two prime ministers of India—Lal Bahadur Shastri and Indira Gandhi—dressed simply and lived in a barn of an old sprawling bungalow. He wore a white lungi and a shirt made of khadi. The shirt's

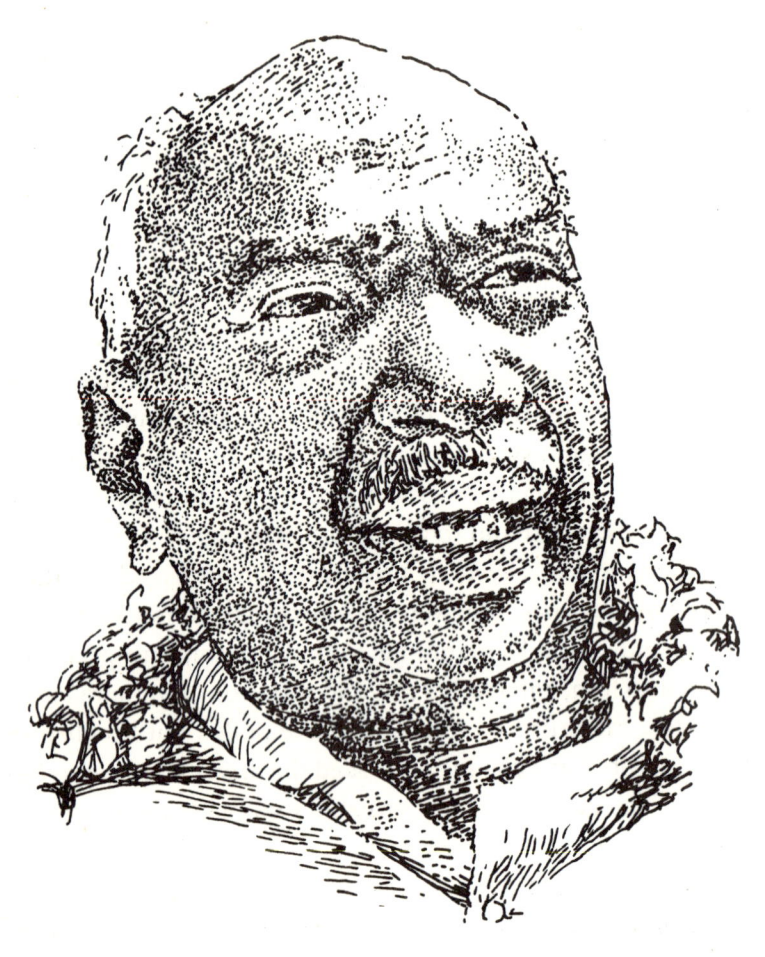

Illustration by Manjula Padmanabhan

distinctive feature was its half sleeves—twice the width of normal half sleeves. The sleeves grew progressively larger, like a trumpet, and were obviously designed to keep him cool in the warm climate of Madras.

For his tall and large frame, his head was quite small. Welles Hangen, author of *After Nehru, Who?* described him aptly, 'Kamaraj, beetle-browed, taciturn and impassive, looks like the captain of a pirate ship.'

It was Kamaraj who provided the answer to the question 'After Nehru, who?' On Nehru's death in 1964, senior leaders in the Congress suggested that Kamaraj should be prime minister. He declined and chose Lal Bahadur Shastri. On Shastri's death, he selected Mrs Indira Gandhi to stand for prime ministership. As captain of the Congress, he steered the party with considerable skill for five years before it split in 1969.

Kamaraj enjoyed absolute power in Tamil Nadu for nearly fifteen years. He practised socialism more than he preached it. When divisive tendencies bubbled up in Madras over the language issue, he made sure the vision of a united India was not lost sight of.

Kamaraj came from a caste of toddy-tappers (Nadars). He was born on 15 July 1903 in the village of Virudhanagar in Ramanad district, Madras state. His father died when he was five years old, and his mother, Sivakamiammal, brought him up. He had only six years of schooling and worked thereafter in his uncle's cloth shop.

The turning point in Kamaraj's life came when he heard Gandhiji speak at Madurai. It was at that moment when the desire to enter politics took hold of him. He had started a shop in Trivandrum but left it in a few months. His first political action was to take part in the salt satyagraha in

1930. He was convicted for two years. As a young volunteer who waved flags and marched in processions, he came under the influence of the Madras leader Satyamurthi, who groomed him for the future leadership of the state Congress. Kamaraj was to achieve this in 1939. He retained the Congress presidentship till 1954, when he became chief minister of Madras state.

Prime Minister Nehru observed that under Kamaraj, Madras was 'the only state which gives me hardly any headache'. In all routine matters, Kamaraj left the decision to civil servants. Though he would be quite willing to collect large funds from industrialists for the Congress, he would refuse to interfere on their behalf in administrative matters unless there was a case of real injustice. Otherwise, he would reply 'Parkalam,' (let us see) and move on.

He left his fellow ministers in charge of the day-to-day work in order to free himself to tour his state twenty days in the month. He was a good listener, heard people's problems and tried to resolve them. He was easily accessible and anyone with a problem could walk into his home till the late hours of the night.

Once torrential rains hit Madras and the slum areas were flooded. Though he was a chief minister, he walked one and a half mile through knee-deep water, organized relief and stayed with slum-dwellers overnight. People still remember that. He introduced midday meals for poor school-children. In the twilight of the Nehru rule, Kamaraj's star was on the ascendant.

Some of the Congress leaders formed a plan which came to be known as the Kamaraj Plan. Kamaraj spelt it out himself as the Congress president: that top leaders of the Congress organization should periodically exchange positions with those in the administration. 'If Congressmen voluntarily accept this free interchange of personnel ... the tendency to form groups in the organizational and legislative wings will be greatly reduced,' he said.

Kamaraj then glowingly referred to the excellent response from senior Congress leaders, many of whom offered to withdraw from ministerial positions, an act which demonstrated, he said, that the spirit of sacrifice and service were not dead. Nehru had earlier accepted the Kamaraj Plan. In the axe that 'voluntarily fell', six chief ministers and six Union ministers, including Morarji Desai and Lal Bahadur Shastri, were 'released for organizational work'. Not all of them went happily and Morarji, number two in the Cabinet, who had submitted his resignation like the rest, was astonished when it was accepted.

The Kamaraj Plan did not result in any organizational revamp but created much heartburn among those who were axed. But it did establish Kamaraj as a force in the Congress.

After Nehru's death, Kamaraj deftly handled the unanimous election of Lal Bahadur Shastri as prime minister. There was no contest, no strife, no regional pressures. The Congress unanimously elected its leader. Those who knew Kamaraj were aware that his loyalty to the Nehru family was so strong that after Shastri's death in January 1966, he would project Mrs Indira Gandhi as his candidate. He did.

Kamaraj was a consummate political chess player but when the DMK wave swept Tamil Nadu in the 1967 elections, he was defeated. Kamaraj was a shaken man. The second blow hit Kamaraj in 1969, when Mrs Gandhi, whom he had installed as prime minister, split the Congress, Kamaraj remaining with the old Congress. The third blow fell on him with the promulgation of the Emergency in 1975.

Although Mrs Gandhi claimed after his death that Kamaraj wanted to bring his Congress party close to hers, the evidence of others contradicts this statement. Those who knew him report how deeply pained he was that many of his old comrades were imprisoned. He died within a few months of the Emergency being declared.

His meteoric rise on the all-India level showed that neither want of education nor lack of a command of English were any bar to growth in political eminence. He was not ambitious for himself, his primary concern was with the party and the country. Contrary to his public image, he could understand English and in private spoke short sentences. My interview with him was translated from Tamil, but I was fortunate enough to hear one of his rare English utterances, 'Regionalism is going up; nationalism is going down.'

He died on 2 October 1975. A contemporary of his wrote, 'Kamaraj belonged to an era when a Congress volunteer was a heroic figure, a man of ideals with a single-minded dedication . . . He enlisted as a humble Congress worker, armed with nothing more than the Gandhian weapon of satyagraha to fight the imperial might. In course of a quarter century of struggle, he spent more than 3,000 days in jail, emerging as a dominant and beloved leader of the Madras state.'

A regional leader, he strode confidently on the national scene, but by the end of his life, he returned to his regional roots where he felt most at home. He died as he lived, a simple bachelor.

K.M. Munshi

I have climbed, no doubt strenuously, but laughing, playing, running.

K.M. Munshi was a littérateur, educationist, lawyer and statesman. His early novels not only captured Gujarat by storm but regenerated its literature. At the height of his career at the Bar, he commanded fabulous fees. Not satisfied with these twin attainments, he went into the sphere of education and founded the Bharatiya Vidya Bhavan, which in his lifetime grew to include twenty-six constituent colleges and their branches. As a statesman, he was at the heart of political affairs for forty years.

In the evening of his life, at eighty-two, his mind was still as sharp as a razor; his cupped ears were alert to catch every word. His reading was wide. He wrote articles and books, and presided and spoke at public occasions wherever possible.

Kanhaiyalal Maneklal Munshi was born at Broach on 30 December 1887. Though he was the son of a government official, his friends got him interested in the Congress session of 1902. 'All my friends were volunteers, but my father would not permit me (to be one),' he said.

'I eat the salt of the British government and I cannot be unfaithful,' said Munshi's father. Cockily, the fifteen-year-old lad replied, 'The salt they give us from our land.' Someone gave Munshi a volunteer's uniform and let him slip into the Congress pandal.

A couple of years later, Russia's defeat by Japan gave a spurt to nationalism in India. In 1905, while at Baroda College, Munshi came under the influence of Professor Aurobindo Ghose, whose ardent nationalism fanned the flame in his heart. Aurobindo at that time believed in terrorism and some of Munshi's young student friends encouraged him to join in the making of bombs. Munshi had hardly started when a crude contraption burst and wounded one of his friends. Munshi promptly decided bombs were not his business. 'I was too much of a coward to go along with it,' he said.

'From 1902 to 1916 I was poor, terribly poor,' Munshi recalled. 'My whole life has been a steep climb; from an eating house costing Rs 5 a month to comparative luxury; from complete obscurity to some recognition. God has indeed been good.'

'People say that you have given a new birth to Gujarati literature. How did you do it?' I asked him.

'I knew neither the grammar nor the syntax of the language, but I knew English well and a little Sanskrit. To it, I added my Broach idiom and the result was a vigorous style freed of classical heaviness,' Munshi said.

'What did you write about?' I asked him.

'About social problems. One of my early novels, *Konno-Vaak* (Whose Fault?), was about a child-widow's life. I wrote about the caste system, of intermarriage, problems not so important now, but vital in those days.'

Some of his historical romances like *Prithvi Vallabh* (The Darling of the Earth) have been made into films. Munshi

Illustration by Manjula Padmanabhan

delved into classical history and the lore of the Puranic period and wrote with feeling. He wrote a series of volumes on Lord Krishna that brought him alive for the modern generation.

Not satisfied with advocating social change, Munshi practised it in his own life. A Brahmin, he married a Jain widow. 'My caste elders were worried. They had looked up to me greatly. When I took such a step, they didn't know what to do. To save them embarrassment, I wrote out a resolution excommunicating myself—which they sadly accepted . . . But I did see the miracle of change in my orthodox mother. She was shocked, but she was so fond of me that she took to my wife, Lilavati.' Lilavati Munshi, who survived him by six years, was herself a well-known novelist and social worker who participated fully in her husband's social and educational endeavours.

In 1914, at the age of twenty-seven, Munshi entered public life and joined Mrs Annie Besant's Home Rule League.

In 1919, he decided to devote himself to legal practice and in the years that followed, he rose to be one of the top lawyers of the land. During these years, he played an active part in the freedom movement and was jailed frequently. He was a close friend of Sardar Patel and became the first home minister of Bombay in 1937. Early in the 1940s, when he saw the movement for Pakistan being launched, he campaigned for an 'Akhand Hindustan' (United India). The Congress officially did not support Munshi's movement but 'Gandhiji blessed me and asked me to work for what I believed, outside the Congress. In spite of my vagaries, he was very kind to me.'

When the Constituent Assembly was formed in 1946, it was Gandhiji who suggested Munshi's name for it. The four years that followed were among the most interesting in Munshi's life. One of the chosen seven, he took to the drafting of the Constitution with zest and thoroughness. Munshi believed in the honour of the pledged word and the sanctity of the Constitution and regretted that it was amended for political popularity like abolishing the Privy Purses of the princes. His book, *Pilgrimage to Freedom*, gives a fascinating account of the independence struggle by a man who had a ringside view and played some part in it.

Few men I have met have had such a passionate love for India. Munshi's great contribution to preserve the country's cultural heritage, the Bharatiya Vidya Bhavan, was born out of this love. For him, India did not mean people living in grinding poverty. His India had the grandeur of Emperor Ashoka who spread the message of love throughout this land and beyond; it was the India of the Mahabharata with its deeds of glory. For Munshi preserved till his last day dreams of Lord Krishna. He had great faith in Hinduism which he did much to revive. Once the question of what is true love came up, and I hesitatingly recommended Henry Drummond's *The Greatest Thing in the World*, which is a Christian's view on love. He later told me how much he appreciated it.

The offices he held were many—including that of Union food minister and Governor of Uttar Pradesh—but it was he who adorned the offices, not the other way round. He was a man of unusual discipline and had a phenomenal dedication to whatever task he took up. It is he who launched the first national campaign for tree planting.

When he was nearing eighty, I went to him somewhat hesitantly at 7 p.m. on a Monday to request him to write an article on a topical constitutional subject for *Himmat* magazine (of which I was editor) by 12 o'clock next morning. It seemed an unfair demand to make on the time and energy of a man of his age who, I knew, always retired at 8 p.m. and woke up at about 8 a.m. He was rather fond of me—as I was of him—and said he would. Next morning his secretary rang up at 11 o'clock. His article was ready, an hour ahead of schedule!

When I inquired how he managed to do it, he said that though with advancing age he slept for long hours, while awake he 'lived intensely every moment'. On the last occasion when I met him, in September 1970, he was eighty-three. He was in his study, correcting a manuscript in large type and treble spacing. In the course of his active life he wrote about 100 books and pamphlets in English and Gujarati, ranging from novels to his authoritative work, *Pilgrimage to Freedom.*

Munshi was a tree that yielded rich fruits. Those who were privileged to have his friendship could find shelter under his shade. His wisdom was always at the disposal of his friends and, to the very last, he was eager to learn. Voracious as a reader, he was prolific as a writer.

Some remember him for his part in drafting the Constitution, some for establishing the Bharatiya Vidya Bhavan, some as a lawyer, a minister or a Governor. But those who knew him intimately remember him as a friend and miss his warmth, wisdom and friendship. In his younger days, he was ambitious and haughty, but later he mellowed to become—when I got to know him—a humble and endearing person. Perhaps this change took place over the years as he evolved from a man of intellect into a man of faith.

Lal Bahadur Shastri

This is my country's call, please do not ask me to ignore it.

The occasion was the laying of the foundation stone of Benares Hindu University. Present on the occasion was a vast concourse of people, including princes who had donated to the university's funds. Invited to lay the foundation stone was a lawyer returned from South Africa who was just making his mark on the land—M.K. Gandhi. He spoke of the shame of a nation suffering under foreign yoke and went on to assail the props of the British Raj, specially the princes. One by one the princes rose and walked out in protest. Officials of the Raj were the next to make their exit. Undeterred, Gandhiji went on. Finally, even the chairman abandoned his post. Gandhiji observed that as the Chair was empty, it was time to conclude his address.

Gandhiji lost the princes and the chairman but he won for life a youngster of eleven years who one day was to wield authority greater than that of all those princes. A few years later Gandhiji issued the call for non-cooperation with British rule and asked students to leave their studies. Lal Bahadur Shastri responded to that call. He was now sixteen. His guru, Mishraji, tried to persuade the young man not to take this hasty step. He appealed to Shastri to think of his widowed mother and sisters. Shastri gently told him, 'This is my country's call. Please do not ask me to ignore it.'

Shastri next went to his mother. 'Please tell me frankly if my action is wrong,' he said. She put her hand on his shoulder. 'I believe in you, son. I also believe that you have not acted in haste and have given good thought to it before taking the step . . . Think well before you decide on a course of action, but once you have taken the step, do not retrace it.'

Equipped with this assurance, Shastri joined the agitation and was arrested in 1921. Shastri's mother, Ramdulari Devi, must have had some premonition about what destiny had in store for her son. When he was four months old, she and her husband went to Allahabad—the holy city of Prayag—for a dip in the Ganges. Crowds pushed and jostled and in this mass of surging humanity, the teenage mother lost grip of her child. And in a flash, he was lost. The baby had tumbled, unknown, into the basket of a milkman. As he had been praying for a child, the milkman thought the baby was an answer to his prayers. Fortunately, the child was soon located and returned to Ramdulari Devi.

About a year later, Shastri's father died. It was his maternal grandfather, Hazari Lal, who showered affection on Shastri who was fondly called Nanhe (small). He grew up in Mugalsarai, not far from Benares. Too poor to afford a football, he and his friends played with a ball made of khajur flowers, wrapped in cloth. A small ball, similarly made, was hit with L-shaped branches, which doubled as their hockey sticks.

After he left studies at Benares Hindu University to participate in the non-cooperation movement, Shastri joined a national university started by Gandhiji's disciples—the Kashi Vidyapeeth. On finishing his four-year course at the

Illustration by Manjula Padmanabhan

Kashi Vidyapeeth, he joined the Servants of the People Society in 1926 for the uplift of the masses. His salary was Rs 60 per month (which came to about Rs 6,000 of 1998).

At twenty-three, he married Lalita Devi. They had four sons and two daughters. Though in later years she travelled with him to Nepal and the Soviet Union, Mrs Shastri maintained, 'My place is in the home.'

In the 1920s and 1930s Shastri participated in the independence movement and made the inevitable rounds of jails. Times were hard. He knew the value of money and even as prime minister, when he left a room, he would make sure that the lights and fans were switched off. It was part of his mental make-up to be thorough which, coupled with his eye for detail and the ability to win people, were responsible for his rise in the Congress hierarchy.

The 'iron in his soul' was nowhere more evident than when he once came home on a week's parole from jail as his four-year-old son was down with typhoid. When the time to return to jail came, the child's temperature had shot up to 106 degrees Fahrenheit. The child whispered, 'Babuji, please don't go.' Tears rolled down Shastri's cheeks. He shook his head, folded his hands to greet everyone, and went back to jail.

During the Quit India period, he was underground for some time, cyclostyling leaflets at Anand Bhavan, Allahabad. He would possibly have escaped detection had he not announced a public meeting, switched the venue and, perching on a tonga, tried to harangue a crowd against the British government. It was not Shastri alone who paid the price of going to jail. With precious little money, his wife bravely tried to bring up a family. She neglected herself and soon contracted tuberculosis. She assured Shastri, then in jail, that all was well. When word reached him about her failing health, Shastri was shaken. He wrote to a friend who looked after Lalita Devi and she got better. Shastri, meanwhile, had lost a lot of weight too. It was a happy reunion when he was released from jail.

After independence, when the Congress came to power, Shastri was elected an MLA and then appointed a minister in the government. For the first time, the family was financially secure. He became, at various times, minister of police, minister for transport and parliamentary secretary to Pandit Pant, the formidable chief minister of Uttar Pradesh. As a minister, he showed his capability and soon Pandit Pant recommended him to Jawaharlal Nehru to take charge of the Congress central election machinery for the first general elections.

So successful was Shastri that he was appointed to oversee the next elections too. By 1962, he, along with Nehru and Indira Gandhi, was one of the three members of the Parliamentary Selection Board. As minister for home affairs, he was close to Nehru. When under the Kamaraj Plan many senior ministers were removed, Nehru reluctantly accepted Shastri's resignation. Not to have done so would have laid him open to the charge that he was favouring Shastri.

Some months later, Nehru had a stroke. Shastri was called to see Nehru and the prime minister asked him for help in disposing his papers. In fact Shastri became Nehru's closest aide as minister without portfolio. In May 1964 when Nehru died Shastri was a strong contender for the prime minister's post. And by a consensus, he was selected by Kamaraj as leader of the Congress Parliamentary Party, and then elected prime minister.

As prime minister, he showed his mettle by handling ably

the language agitation in the south; India's relations with her neighbours; the war—and subsequent peace—with Pakistan.

When Tamil Nadu was in turmoil over the imposition of Hindi, Shastri, coming from the heart of Hindi-speaking India, assured the people that Hindi would not be imposed on them and that English would continue as an associate language.

Shastri's visits to Nepal helped to heal a rupture between India and the mountain kingdom. He went to Sri Lanka to discuss the problems of plantation workers of Indian origin and settled the issue. Next, he visited Burma.

But the dominating issue was India's relations with Pakistan. Perhaps mistaking Shastri's gentleness for weakness, President Ayub Khan made armed intrusions into the Kutch frontier and some months later threw in the full weight of the Pakistan army into Kashmir.

Pakistan was confident that India would not dare to cross the international border into Punjab. Shastri took them by surprise when he approved of the Indian army's plan to cross the international border. Within no time, the Indian army was on the outskirts of Lahore and Sialkot. During that short war, the tiny Indian Gnats proved more successful than the large but less manoeuvrable US Sabre jets. At a rally in Bombay, before a crowd of almost a million, Shastri spoke with a light touch. Looking diminutive as he stood on a high podium, he told the rally about the Gnats, adding, 'These days it seems, it is the little things which prove more effective!' The audience roared with approval as the little man said those words.

The war over, Shastri told his Cabinet colleagues, 'Now we must preserve peace with the same vigour with which we pursued the war.'

Four months after the war, at the Hall of the Sessions at Tashkent, Shastri discussed the Indo-Pak differences with President Ayub Khan, and under the aegis of Prime Minister Kosygin of the USSR, a historic declaration was signed. The two nations agreed to withdraw from all territories occupied during the war and not to resort to force to resolve problems. Both reiterated their stand on Kashmir but no more.

That night at 10 o'clock Shastri rang up his family to find out the reaction to the agreement in India. A couple of hours later, as he was unwinding after the strenuous negotiations of the previous days, he had a heart attack. Before the doctors could help him, he was no more. At his finest hour, the hero of India had fallen.

Next morning, a sorrowing nation received Shastri's body. Millions felt as if one of their own family members had passed away. Shastri had none of the glamour of Nehru or the terrific mass appeal of Gandhiji, and yet he had in eighteen short months endeared himself to the nation. A few days later, it became common knowledge that Shastri had left little money and had taken a bank loan.

How did Shastri manage to endear himself the way he did? He had the common touch. Shastri had no fanciful thoughts. He touched no heights of oratory. He was of the earth. He had an art so rare among politicians—the ability to laugh at himself. His great joy was to play with his grandchildren. Once he is reported to have complained, 'I am so small that nobody likes to play with me. I therefore turn to children.'

In 1958, when he was Union railway minister, I went to see him with some young men who had decided to set their lives aright for the nation's sake. He looked tiny seated in that ministerial high chair. One of the young men spoke of how he had stopped travelling by public transport without tickets. Shastri bent forward and said quite simply, 'You know, I too used to do the same. I had no money as a young man and at one time I used to journey daily in the train without a ticket!' He recalled that the distance he covered was about eighteen miles a day. When the young men stepped out of his chamber, they felt that they had met a man who could understand them.

That gift of understanding he brought to his statesmanship. He was never harsh or dogmatic but had a mind of his own. 'There is more iron in his soul than appears on the surface,' commented former US Ambassador John Kenneth Galbraith. 'He listens to every point of view, he makes up his mind firmly, and once he has made them, his decisions stick . . . He is the kind of man who is trusted.'

Shastri had that rarest of qualities among politicians, the ability to love even those who disagreed with him. The Opposition did not relish attacking him personally. His friend and biographer, D.R. Mankekar, in his biography, *Lal Bahadur Shastri,* wrote glowingly about him,

> When he spoke, his large soft eyes looked into you; and his soothing voice at once put you at ease and spoke to you as a brother and not as a superior person—no self-conceit, no vain glory, no ego-centricity, the most common failing in a political celebrity. Shastri was the most human personality this writer ever came across. For after fashioning Shastri, Nature would appear to

have broken the mould. There is none other like him.

Those who had met Shastri would agree with this assessment.

Minoo Masani

The fight for bread and freedom has of course to be waged simultaneously. We want both for our people—we want bread through freedom because it is the only way to get it.

In the early years of the twentieth century, at the fishing village of Versova, Bombay, was a creek. Upon its shore was a notice, 'Swimming here is dangerous.' Many people had been dragged into the sea while braving the strong currents at ebb tide. Undeterred, a young boy braved the currents almost daily. On some occasions, as he swam vigorously, he felt he was losing the battle against the current, and he could see the Versova shore recede. Then would follow, Minoo Masani recalls, 'the triumph of survival, of throwing oneself in the sand, all spent, and gradually regaining one's breath'.

Swimming against the tide became a habit with him. When India was under the Raj, he fought the British and was imprisoned three times. When India became free, he dared to stand up to his old friend Jawaharlal Nehru who, he felt, was taking India on the road to state capitalism. Masani visited the Soviet Union in 1927 and was charmed by what he saw. He urged Nehru to visit the Soviet Union, which Nehru did. Later, Masani was disillusioned by the Soviet Union under Stalin. Nehru's admiration continued. And Masani became a bitter critic of Nehru—one of the first.

A man of varied talents, Masani was a co-founder, with J.P. and others, of the Congress Socialist Party; mayor of Bombay; author; journalist; and a member of the Constituent Assembly and the Parliament. In the early 1940s, he became famous for his book, *Our India*, on which a whole generation grew up, inspired by his love of and a vision for India. In the late forties, he sat in the Constituent Assembly and was involved in drafting the Constitution of India. In 1950, Dr John Matthai sounded him out for the office of food minister under Nehru. In 1948, Masani was appointed as ambassador to Brazil.

In 1959, Rajaji, aware of Masani's organizing skills, requested him to be the general secretary of the newly formed Swatantra Party. In nine years he forged it into the largest Opposition party and became the leader of the Opposition in the Lok Sabha. J.R.D. Tata warned him, 'Minoo, the trouble with you is that you cannot suffer fools, and in politics you have to.' When Minoo started the Swatantra Party, he was prepared for fools but he did not reckon that in his party and among the Opposition leaders, he would also encounter a fair share of knaves. When other politicians were keen to forge a grand coalition to defeat Mrs Gandhi at the polls in 1971, Masani was unpopular with politicians for insisting on an agreed programme before the elections. Predictably, they could not frame any and lost the elections. Minoo resigned from the presidentship of the Swatantra Party in 1971. Later, much against his advice, the party was merged with the Jat leader Charan Singh's Bharatiya Kranti Dal (BKD). And the Swatantra Party melted out of politics.

Looking back at his political career of forty years, was it all a waste of time then? In reply, Masani quoted the poet Arthur Hugh Clough (1819–61) in his autobiography:

Illustration by Gautam Roy

Say not, the struggle naught availeth,
The labour and the wounds are vain,
The enemy faints not, nor faileth,
And as things have been they remain . . .

For while the tired waves, vainly breaking
Seem here no painful inch to gain,
Far back, through creeks and inlets making,
Come silent, flooding in, the main.

Masani added, 'Whether mine is a life of wasted opportunities, I do not know, but it is a life I would live again.'

Masani was born in Bombay on 20 November 1905. Son of a distinguished civil servant and author, Sir Rustom Masani, Minoo in his early years studied at Cathedral School. His principal, Mr Savage, was true to his name and though Masani escaped his canings, he could not escape hammering by the bullies in the school. This, however, served to toughen him. He was shifted to Bharda New High School and later joined Elphinstone College. As a child he was called 'Mr Why' because he always pestered his parents for an explanation for everything, not a bad start for one who was to join the London School of Economics, whose motto is *Rerum Cognoscere Causas* (To know the cause of things).

In those formative years when H.G. Wells and Bernard Shaw wielded enormous influence, Masani was inspired by them and became an iconoclast like them.

He passed his Bar exam. On return to India in 1928, Masani joined the chambers of Mr F. Coltman at the Bar but the call of politics, as stated by his close friend, Yusuf Meherally, drew him into the Civil Disobedience movement.

He was arrested and confined in Nasik jail in 1933 where many eminent men like J.P., Achyut Patwardhan, Asoka Mehta and Yusuf Meherally were incarcerated. When they came out of jail in 1934, they launched the Congress Socialist Party with Nehru's blessings, though not his association. Nehru and young Masani were quite close to each other. Masani stayed with him and Kamala Nehru. He would recall later that Jawaharlal was always very kind to her.

Sir Rustom Masani, one of the first Indians to be the municipal commissioner of Bombay, did not take very kindly to the anti-British and pro-Socialist activities of his son. Sensibly, Minoo left home so as not to embarrass his father. Speaking about his life he related how he got a low-paid job in *Janmabhoomi* newspaper and he, who once ate dinners at Middle Temple, now had to make do with bread and butter in Cecil Restaurant at Hughes Road. He could not afford a lavish meal. It was when he was in this impoverished state that he wrote *Our India* which inaugurated a new chapter in Indian publishing and was the first book by an Indian author to sell 1,00,000 copies. In later editions, 6,50,000 copies of the book were sold. In the early forties, the book popularized the concept of planning. The skies cleared for Masani. Tatas offered him a job. When not very active in political life, he had a fruitful time in Tatas, at one time in 1954 being the Chef de Cabinet to J.R.D. Tata.

Though as Socialists the young men tried to convert Gandhiji to their ideas, the magician was making a greater impression on these young men than they had on him. Ten days of daily walks in the 1930s with the Mahatma had already made an impact on Masani.

In 1944, Masani published *Socialism Reconsidered*, which made many of his old friends furious. The Soviet

Revolution had disillusioned Masani. He modestly claimed that his book anticipated a great deal of the thesis of Yugoslav political leader and writer, Milovan Djilas's *The New Class*, published in 1956. It took time for Jayaprakash Narayan to be critical of Marxism but for years, Masani tried to influence him, for example, once he sent J.P. Arthur Koestler's *Darkness at Noon* which revealed the darker side of Stalinist rule.

In the Constituent Assembly, Masani was in the Fundamental Rights Sub-Committee and sensed the glory and the challenge of shaping the India of the future. Ambedkar, Masani, Hansa Mehta and Rajkumari Amrit Kaur wanted a common civil code for all Indians, including Muslims, but many others turned it down.

Nehru spoke approvingly to J.P. about Masani's role in the Constituent Assembly but found him a nuisance on his return from Brazil. Repeatedly, Masani took a stand contrary to Nehru and they drifted apart.

For Masani, 'the central problem of our time is whether the state is to own the people or the people are to own the state'. On this fundamental issue, articulated by him in the Constituent Assembly, he fought a consistent battle. All else he did politically flowed from it. Freedom, in his view, came first. Once you subordinated it, the slide knew no limit. In the 1960s, he started a monthly magazine, appropriately called *Freedom First*. In 1968, with J.R.D. Tata's help, he started the Leslie Sawhny Programme for Training in Democracy. He nurtured it with care and abounding zeal in spite of his other political preoccupations. Though a passionate lover of freedom and democracy, he could be quite authoritarian in his ways. In his last years he threw himself (some might say overboard) in his 'Right to Die' Campaign of which he was world president.

Masani had one supreme quality. He was never neutral, and no one could be neutral towards him. Either you liked Minoo or you didn't. He saw people in terms of good or bad; with the good being those who were 'politically sound' and those who, in the game of politics, were principled.

Some saw Masani as a cold, aloof figure, a 'Mister Always Right'—Right in more ways than one. But as sometimes happens, behind the dazzling brilliance of his intellect lay a heart which once it gave its loyalty to someone, could be solicitous and considerate. But it was also perhaps a heart that was hurt and hence was well-hidden. In two volumes of his racy autobiography there is hardly anything about his two marriages which were not too successful and there is no more than a passing reference to his only son, Zareer, who wrote a biography of Indira Gandhi at a time when his father was battling Mrs Gandhi over the issue of censorship during the Emergency.

Masani had considerable influence on J.P. and was all too conscious of it. Once Masani was discussing a matter with J.P. and was visibly upset at the stand J.P. was taking. Knowing his closeness to J.P., I asked him, 'But why don't you get J.P. to do it?' 'No', replied Masani. 'He does not think the same way, and for me to try to force him would be committing violence against him.' In these words Masani redefined for me the meaning of violence as well as of true friendship.

His sharp and over-critical intellect made him respect few leaders but for four people he had unbounded admiration—Gandhiji, Rajaji, J.P. and J.R.D. Tata.

Perhaps in any other country Masani would have held high office. In some ways he was so Indian and in other ways quite un-Indian. For example, he was remarkably disciplined. In his eight months of imprisonment at Nasik, he read 100 books—more than most politicians have touched in their lifetime! I was struck when once at Bombay airport he opened his briefcase, pulled out some of the latest journals and started underlining as he read. He was time conscious like Gandhiji. In Bihar, when a deputation of his partymen who had come to meet him were ten minutes late, he looked at his watch, glowered, and said, 'You have made me lose my ten minutes.' They looked at each other, baffled. He could not adjust to the reality that in Bihar if anyone came within the hour of his appointment, one would rejoice at the sight of the visitor.

Incidentally, his brother, Dr Keki Masani, a psychiatrist, seldom came on time while he was a professor at the Tata Institute of Social Sciences. The students had composed a ditty for Keki:

Our poor Dr Masani has a sad fate,
However hard he tries, he is always late.

A brother of Minoo's who was a mathematician worked in the US. His sister, Mehra, a gracious lady, retired as director-general of the All India Radio and helped Minoo with the Leslie Sawhny Endowment Programme.

A champion of freedom, Masani fought two cases of national importance. When the Bank Nationalization Ordinance was proclaimed, it was he, with Nani Palkhivala and friends, who took the issue to the Supreme Court. Again, during the Emergency, it was he who refused to submit proofs of his paper, *Freedom First*, for precensorship. The Bombay High Court ruled in his favour, rejecting precensorship, thereby helping others to keep the torch of free speech burning.

Masani gave ample evidence of his uncanny ability to foresee the political future. In March 1975, as J.P.'s agitation gained momentum, Masani read out to J.P. an excerpt from his forthcoming book, *Is J.P. the Answer?*

> An outright victory might only be possible for those in office by a seizure of power and the establishment of a dictatorship, accompanied perhaps by more brutal repression than anything British rule had perpetrated in this country.

That was three months before the Emergency. He suggested Indira Gandhi accept J.P. as a colleague.

He wrote:

> Would not then sharing power with Jayaprakash, a comrade in the struggle for independence and a friend of her father's, be a much more attractive alternative, whether from the national or personal point of view? Of course it would mean not being surrounded any longer by stooges and flatterers. Of course it would mean the end of tolerating corrupt colleagues. Of course it would mean a parting of ways with the communists. Most revolutions exact from those in power a much higher price than this. In return, there would be the reward of popular affection in place of bitterness and comradeship in place of confrontation.

The book was published in May 1975. Indira Gandhi did not heed him. The Emergency was declared on 25 June 1975.

Sometime in June 1977 I had another evidence of Masani's prescience. He called me over to see an article he had written for a foreign journal on the Janata government, then hardly three months in power. I read the article. It was too critical in parts. I thought perhaps it was premature and the government deserved more time. Graciously, he accepted my viewpoint. Time was to prove him right and me wrong.

In his mid-eighties he married, for the third time, Sheila Singh, who had worked with him for twenty years in the Leslie Sawhny Programme for Training in Democracy. It was the happiest of his marriages. As twilight descended and he was nearing ninety, he said how well she—much younger to him—looked after him. It was sad to see him after ninety. First, his vision was impaired and then his mind, once sparkling, slowed down, and his brilliance and memory faded. He hardly spoke.

In reply to a letter of condolence, Sheila Masani wrote, 'Minoo would have lived to be a hundred, so robust was his constitution but for the fact that the most cherished part of his self started giving way—his sight. This began some years ago but the best of doctors were helpless. And, as his ability to read and write started giving way, so did his zest for living.

'Minoo is gone but his courage in standing up and being counted even if he was in a minority of one, his spirit of dissent, will be with me and with all those who were close to him.'

In his adolescence Masani started swimming against the tide. He continued to do so all his life. In 1998 when in his nineties, Masani expired after a prolonged battle with illness.

Morarji Desai

*My father's death when I was fifteen, was also a blessing
. . . because I would have never ceased to be a coward if
my father had not gone.*

Of all the personalities featured in this book, no one suffered from my pen as much as Morarji Desai did. Almost fifty years ago, when he was the home and chief minister of Bombay and I a young journalist in my early twenties, I attacked him with verve and vigour for what I thought was his autocratic conduct as Home Minister and later as Chief Minister of Bombay State. To my knowledge the facts I had gathered were correct, but my sharp comments were geared to wound him. After seeing a play of Moral Re-Armament called *The Real News*, I wrote a letter of apology to him for the personal hurt I had caused him. Taken aback, he told the then mayor of Bombay, 'See what these journalists are! The man attacks me in public, and apologizes to me in private!' Fortunately, my editor, D.F. Karaka, to whom I had sent a copy of my letter, wrote a two-column editorial in *Current* criticizing me for my apology. After reading this, Morarji Desai wrote a courteous letter in which he said, 'I hope you will agree that criticism to be effective should aim at the deed and not at the doer.'

Eight years later, in 1962, Morarji accompanied

Illustration by Manjula Padmanabhan

Jawaharlal Nehru to the Commonwealth Prime Ministers' Conference. I rang him from the foyer of London's Claridge's Hotel one morning.

'You won't remember me, my name is R.M. Lala,' I said.

'I remember you very well,' came the firm reply.

'I wonder whether I can see you sometime,' I asked.

'Come up to my room,' he said.

I opened the tall, pale green door of his VIP suite. As I surveyed the vast light-green sitting room, furnished with gold brocade chairs and sofas, no one was visible seated on any of them. As I was wondering if I had come to the wrong place, a voice came from the far end. Morarji Desai, the finance minister of India, the man expected to succeed Nehru, was squatting on the floor at a distance, spinning away. He was perhaps the first and the last man to spin at Claridge's.

My second meeting with Morarji was in April 1963. He had moved the controversial Gold Control Order in Parliament and was in an aggressively defiant mood. The talk centred round Moral Re-Armament. Though accepting that there was a change in me, he maintained, 'People don't change that easily,' and continued on this theme for awhile. Somewhat exasperated I, then only thirty-five, said, 'Morarjibhai, when you experience a change in your own life and heart, you will know people can change.' There was dead silence. I expected him to show me the door. I deserved it but he sat in silence scratching his newly shaven head. We then changed the subject.

I continued to see him occasionally over the years. When I saw him one afternoon in April 1980 at his residence at Marine Drive, the offices of home and chief minister of Bombay, of Union finance minister, deputy prime minister, and prime minister lay behind him. At eighty-five, he sat erect against the mattress, writing letters by hand. On the table beside him lay a bottle of almonds and rock sugar. In the intervening years, between my meeting with him at Claridge's and the Marine Drive, his fortunes had dipped twice and twice did they revive. Neither the fury of his colleagues and opponents, nor the accident of a plane crash in Assam, nor the crumbling of his Cabinet, seemed to have made any difference to his unflappable ways. That afternoon India's most enduring politician recalled his years of prime ministership and of his childhood. From one, he flashed back to the other, drawing some links between the two. His Janata Cabinet (1977-79), he claimed, 'had functioned very well'.

'Then why did it break up within two and a half years?' I asked.

'It is inherent in the nature of this country,' he replied. 'We have inherited for centuries a fear complex. When a man is afraid, he does many wrong things to save himself. From fear come lies, from fear come deceit and selfishness. We are afraid of every little thing, even to tell one's friend that he has done something wrong because he will take it ill . . . Unless you give up fear, you cannot be truthful. And unless you are truthful, you cannot give up fear. Once you master fear and untruth, you give up selfishness. Lies go with fear; truth with fearlessness.'

'Is that why you often speak of fearlessness?'

'I have done that because I suffered from fear as a young boy till I was sixteen. I was afraid of every little thing.'

'What happened to change your life?'

It happened that Morarji Desai's father was an impoverished but principled school master in Bulsar, Gujarat, who earned Rs 40 per month. He was not given a promotion for seven years but was too proud to flatter anybody to gain it. One evening, as the family settled down to dinner, waiting for the father to join them, they heard a thud in the distance. They ran to the well to discover that he had committed suicide.

'The whole burden of the family came upon me at fifteen because I was the eldest. No income and a family of nine to maintain. And I was in the matriculation class. At that time I resolved not to beg from anybody and not to incur any debt. And this gave me fearlessness.'

'How did you support your family?'

Morarji related that his maternal grandfather was of some help. Morarji was awarded a scholarship to G.T. School in Bombay which looked after his boarding, lodging and studies and gave him a monthly allowance of Rs 10. Morarji gave tuitions to earn extra money, never used public transport, and walked everywhere he had to travel. He saved each paisa and sent it to his family. This experience was the making of the man.

'When I went to college at sixteen, I think in the very first year I lost fear. This enabled me to pass through all kinds of difficulties. You see, my father's death was also a blessing from that point of view because I would have never ceased to be a coward if my father had not gone. What God does, we never know. We must take it as a blessing, whatever he does.'

'Were you very fond of your father?'

'He was also fond of me. He gave me the strength of independence of spirit.'

At Wilson College, Bombay, Morarji says he was 'very sensitive and very poor'. At that age, he was not above playing tricks. He remembers with affection his principal, Rev. Dr Scott. Affection, however, did not prevent Morarji from getting the better of the learned Scotsman. 'We had compulsory Bible study in the first hour and were marked present just before that. Dr Scott used to take that class. It was a big room on the second floor with a platform at one end and I always sat at the other end. Both had exit doors and I was the nearest to the exit at the far end. One staircase was near the principal's platform and the other at my end. When the principal prayed, he used to close his eyes and that was the moment for me to slip away. One day he must have seen me, so the next day, he opened his eyes as I moved out. He jumped from the platform and ran down two flights of stairs to catch me. But I saw him jumping so I went back to my seat. Dr Scott ran down the stairs and came up out of breath to find me sitting undisturbed in the classroom! What could he do?' chuckled Morarji.

In college, Morarji got high marks. He badly needed a job. A professor friend of his filled an application form for the Provincial Civil Service and got him to sign it. Called to the interview, he went in his friend's borrowed clothes.

Three English ICS Secretaries interviewed him. At the end of the interview, one of them said, 'Well, young man, if you are not selected, how would you feel?' Morarji replied, 'India is vast. I am young. Who knows, I may get something better!' Many years later, Morarji was told that his reply greatly impressed the panel and though all the vacancies had been filled, they created an extra post for him. Morarji resigned from the service of the British government after about twelve years, when he was a deputy collector in 1930. He threw himself into the national movement. Between 1937 and 1957 many high offices came his way. He was revenue minister, home minister and chief minister of the undivided and huge state of Bombay. Nehru took him to Delhi in 1957, and in less than five years Morarji, as the finance minister, was number two in the Cabinet. Under the Kamaraj Plan of 1963 he tendered his resignation along with others and, to his surprise, Nehru accepted it. When Nehru died a year later, Morarji made a bid for premiership. Congress president Kamaraj took a consensus and outbid him by appointing Lal Bahadur Shastri as the prime minister. When Shastri died, Kamaraj proposed Mrs Gandhi's name as leader of the party. This time, Morarji insisted on a contest. He stood but lost. J.P. once drew my attention to the fact that with the entire Congress leadership supporting Mrs Gandhi, Morarji still managed to get a third of the votes cast.

Twelve years later, in March 1977, on the crest of the Janata wave, the office that had eluded him came his way. The Janata was a coalition of parties and as in any such arrangement, the disparate views and aspirations of the constituents ensured that the premiership was not a bed of roses. 'When did the trouble first start in the Cabinet?' I inquired.

'It started from the very beginning but I patiently went on. Charan Singh told me, "I made you prime minister and you are not doing this . . ."'

Charan Singh, the number two man in Morarji's Cabinet and an aspirant for prime ministership himself, handed in his resignation but Morarji brought him back. Ironically, Morarji was jockeyed out of his post as prime minister by Charan Singh in 1979.

'If you had a chance all over again, would you do anything differently?' I asked Morarji.

'I should not have taken Charan Singh back into the Cabinet. I knew I should not have but when my colleagues were of the view . . .'

'So you yielded.'

'Warning them that it would have a disastrous result. And it did.'

In a lighter mood, he added that when he became prime minister he was eighty-two and his political peers thought 'I would pass away and one of them would succeed me. Then President Sanjiva Reddy told them, "He will survive you all." That took away the patience of Charan Singh!'

Morarji laughed heartily at this point.

'Did you expect your resignation would come so soon? Was it escalated?'

'No, I expected it would come any time.'

'What was your greatest disappointment as prime minister?'

'I take things as they come. I don't run the world, the world is run by its Maker and not by me and it follows certain irrevocable laws. The results are according to these laws. One must make one's best effort to get results.'

I have seen Morarji Desai while he was holding high office and also during times of defeat. In defeat, he was dauntless. In success, some have felt the lash of his arrogant words. The time when I got to know him best was between 1964 and 1967, when he had missed the premiership on two occasions. I can picture him in those years in his modest New Delhi home, seated on a mattress on the floor, with his back to the empty fireplace, surrounded by books—rather bulky volumes of Vivekananda. His tiny white transistor broadcast a cricket commentary while his hands were busy at his spinning wheel. He was in political wilderness then. 'It is good for me,' he said. So did his opponents!

For decades Morarji's routine was unvarying. He woke up by 5 o'clock every morning and before the city could stir, he had had his bath, recited the Gita (which he knew by heart), and finished his exercises. He was a man of prodigious energy, considerable achievement and had an opinion on every subject. He could be witty, wise and philosophical, drawing upon his considerable knowledge of the Hindu scriptures. Sometimes he appeared subdued, almost morose. At other times, he would entertain people to a lively discourse. He was quick at repartee, and, at times, tended to be abrupt to the point of rudeness. If Dale Carnegie refined the art of winning friends, Morarji refined the art of losing them.

Morarji was a complex mixture of a tough, worldly politician and a seeker of things of the spirit. The lesser known side of him was that of a person endeavouring to be a spiritual superman. He once told me, 'Even physical pain does not bother me. I can smile with that pain.' When I remarked it was easier to say this than to practise it, he replied, 'You have to pay a price for it. I know it is not easy, I have taken years to achieve it.'

Many of Morarji's friends sometimes wished that he would allow himself to be more human and frail. Had he done that, India's most enduring politician could perhaps have been its most endearing.

I once ventured to tell Morarji that if he would allow himself to show people that he could be frail and human, their hearts would go out to him. 'Is frailty a virtue?' he shot back defiantly.

Waiting at Morarji's home once, I had a long chat with his wife, Gajraben. I could sense how deeply she felt her husband's political problems. When she died, I told him, 'She was a good woman.' For once the mask was off Morarji. 'Yes,' he replied gently with resignation in his voice. 'She was a good woman.'

On his ninety-ninth birthday, there was a celebration on the terrace of his house. Rich tributes were paid. Morarji was as stoic as ever. A few months later in 1995, he passed away.

Mother Teresa

If you judge people, you have no time to love them.

The blue-and-white stripes of her sari framed her lined and smiling face. Mother Teresa stood in the corridor outside her chapel in Lower Circular Road, Calcutta, shorter in height than I had imagined her to be. A coachload of tourists were crowding around her and she had a word for each one. They were pushing currency notes into her left hand and clicking their cameras. She was unfazed by both. She was more interested in the people who crowded in front of her. Every time she had even a brief word with one of the tourists, her eyes seemed to dwell entirely on him or her. As the tourist guide gave the call that they should leave for the airport, she gently asked, 'Would you not like to spend some time with Jesus in our Chapel?' Meekly, they trooped in. She looked upon herself mainly as a channel that took people to God.

Agnes Gonxha Bejaxhiu was born on 26 August 1910, of Albanian parents. She grew up in Skopje, Yugoslavia, where her parents had settled. At the age of twelve, Agnes wanted to become a nun, and at eighteen she joined the Order of Loreto nuns. At the age of nineteen, she arrived in India. When asked what influences shaped her life, she simply replied, 'Love of parents and the Gospels.' When I pressed the question, asking if any book or perhaps any Catholic saint had particularly

Illustration by Manjula Padmanabhan

influenced her, she shook her head.

'Why did you choose India for your service?' I asked her.

'Because India was a missionary country like the countries of Africa,' Mother Teresa replied.

For over six decades India was the arena of her life and work. She became an Indian citizen in 1948.

'Do you have any relatives at home?' I inquired.

'No,' she replied, 'only a brother.' Some sentiment seemed to sweep over her. She visibly pulled herself up at that stage and requested me to change the subject.

'I love teaching most of all,' she said, and she gave seventeen years of her life to it. At one time she was principal of St. Mary's High School, Calcutta. Many of the girls who joined her in the early years were her pupils. The girls in the school came from well-to-do families and were neatly dressed. She saw them a good part of the day, but when she came to her room, she saw the horrors of Moti Jheel slum nearby. The squalor made her spirit uneasy, and in her many retreats she sought an answer to this restlessness.

One day while she was on a train speeding to Darjeeling she heard the answer to her prayers. 'I heard the call to give up all and follow Him into the slums, to serve Him amongst the poorest of the poor.'

'You accepted what the Inner Voice asked of you?' Malcolm Muggeridge, renowned author, once inquired of her.

'I knew it was His will,' she replied, 'and that I had to follow Him. There was no doubt it was going to be His work. But I waited for the decision of the Church.'

Mother Teresa never doubted that it was God's calling for her.

I questioned her years later, in 1979, 'How does a person

know for sure what his or her calling is?'

She replied, 'Deep down in our heart we know exactly what our calling is—if we are humble and sincere. God cannot deceive us. He created us to love and to be loved. He created us for deeper things. There is some hand, some purpose, behind our being.'

The decision of the church took almost a couple of years. When she got the Pope's permission, she left the neat lawns of Loreto and the life she knew for the rigours of the unknown way. She exchanged the habit of the nun and donned a coarse sari with blue striped borders. She first went to Patna for a three-month intensive course in nursing. Then with Rs 5 and plenty of faith she launched out into her work. She visited the homes of the poor in Calcutta. She saw the need of a school for children and started with five youngsters. They were grown-up kids but she had to begin with the Bengali alphabets. There was no blackboard, so she wrote the alphabets in the dust.

Next day, two or three girls from Loreto came to help her with the children, and so the work started. They found one room to live in, in the home of a generous family. But soon they needed two rooms. And so the work grew.

The first woman whom Mother Teresa picked up from the streets was half eaten by rats and ants. The hospital admitted her only because Mother Teresa refused to budge. On the same day she found other people dying on the streets. She went to the municipal authorities for a place. They offered her a rest-house for pilgrims who came to the Kali temple. It was an empty building and Mother Teresa was delighted to receive it. Within twenty-four hours, she had patients there, and since then she and her nuns have picked up about 50,000 people, of whom about half have died.

'We help the poor to die with God,' she says. 'We help them to say sorry to God. It is between them and God alone. Nobody else. Nobody has the right to come in at that time. We just help them to make peace with God. We live that they may die in peace, so that they may go home according to what is written in the Book, be it written according to Hindu or Muslim or Buddhist or Catholic or Protestant or any other people. There are societies that collect their own dead. We have never had any trouble.'

She called her first home for the dying Nirmal Hriday, meaning 'place of the pure heart'. Nobody there has died feeling unwanted or unloved. She called that home 'the treasure house of Calcutta'. Some who are dying ask for Ganges water, others for a prayer, some ask for an apple or a cigarette. Others simply want somebody to sit with them as they go.

As she launched upon this work, she encountered opposition. A group of young people began to go round threatening to chase the nuns out. The nuns were naturally frightened. Some of the young people had earlier convinced the police commissioner of the need to chase Mother Teresa out of the locality. On arrival, the police commissioner found the Mother cleaning sores from a wound infected with maggots. The stench was unbearable. He went back to the young people and said, 'I have given my word that I will push this lady out, and I will keep it. But before I do, you must get your mothers and your sisters to do the work she is doing. Only then will I exercise my authority.' The crowd melted away, but the attacks continued.

One day she confronted these wild people, 'If this is the way you want it, kill me. I will go straight to Heaven. But you must stop this nonsense.' After that the attacks stopped. 'I don't do it. He does it,' she said. 'I am only an instrument in his hand.'

From that one Home have now sprung up scores of Homes for the dying destitutes around the world, run by the Missionaries of Charity. To the three normal vows of chastity, poverty and obedience, she added a fourth: 'Whole-hearted free service to the poorest of the poor.'

Mother Teresa's second focus of attention were abandoned children. She kept an open door for children, whether they were hopeless cases from hospitals or jails, or were abandoned infants dumped in dustbins. To her abortion was not only murder but was also man or woman putting himself or herself in the place of God, deciding whether life should survive. 'Our way is to preserve life; the life of Christ in the child.' Today, the Order runs over fifty Homes for abandoned children. One of the toddlers whom the sisters had picked up was asked what he would like to become when he grew up. He confidently replied, 'I will become Mother Teresa.' When he was old enough, the Mother sent him for training in priesthood.

The third great thrust of Mother Teresa's work was for the lepers. In 1957, five lepers came to her Home. Fortunately, by then a doctor had joined her in the work. At one time, there were 10,000 lepers under the care of the Missionaries of Charity. Her Sisters are specially trained for this work, and many times if the patients came early enough, are able to find a cure. When Mother Teresa started her first Home for lepers in Calcutta, a municipal councillor objected, because the place was situated near his home, and he turned the Municipal Corporation against her venture. Not one to give up so easily, Mother Teresa had a bright idea; instead of having a fixed centre, could she have a mobile dispensary?

She turned the obstacle into a stepping stone. She told the objector, 'Bless you, councillor, you have increased our efficiency a hundred times.' There are now almost 500 mobile dispensaries run by the Missionaries of Charity. In addition, there is a spacious colony for lepers at Shantinagar (Abode of Peace) on land given to Mother Teresa by the West Bengal Government.

What was it that made it possible for the Mother and her Sisters to do the kind of work normally nobody volunteers to do? Frequently, she quoted the words, 'I was hungry and you fed Me, I was naked and you clothed Me, I was sick and you visited Me, I was homeless and you took Me in. Whatever you did, you did it to Me.' On this motivation her work was based. For her, it was a privilege to tend to the sick.

When I observed to Mother Teresa that it could be said that she dealt with the outward manifestations of poverty, but not with the root, which is the selfishness and cruelty that creates poverty, she promptly replied, 'Poverty is man-made and not made by God. That is why Jesus became man to experience it. But for those who are consecrated (to the work), poverty is a joy and a freedom. If you talk of cruelty, you are judging others and meanwhile someone who needs help may die in the next two hours. If you judge people, you have no time to love them.'

For a journalist trained to judge and write, these were strong words that have rung in my ears ever since.

It dawned on me that behind this woman of action lay a whole value system that could be the structure of a new civilization. Her scale of values was so utterly different from the world's, and yet the mighty and the affluent were drawn to her because she symbolized the inner life we all hunger for. While philosophers, at best, write books, she raised a force of people spanning the globe, applying cheerfully in action her beliefs—at a price to themselves.

Mother Teresa thought profoundly on matters of life and death. Unlike many of us, in her value system there was no gap between words and action. They were all of one piece. Her power came from an integrated personality.

If she criticized abortion, she did not stop at just attacking abortion as 'a terrible sin'. She would go to the dustbins, retrieve the abandoned infants and struggle for their survival. If her mission was to serve 'the poorest of the poor', she was equally concerned about rich Westerners. I could see it in her eyes as she talked to the tourists. If the poor feel unwanted, so do the affluent. The loneliness of the Westerners touched her as much as that of the dying destitutes on the streets of Calcutta. Hers was a conscience finely tuned to the world's suffering. 'Loneliness,' she once observed, 'is worse than poverty.'

For her, material acquisitions were for one purpose only, to relieve suffering and bring people closer to God. Passing by the marble grandeur of the Victoria Memorial in Calcutta, with its statue of Queen Victoria at one end and of Lord Curzon on the other, she sighed longingly and mentioned how wonderful it would be if she could use this monument for the poor.

According to her the biggest disease in the world today was feeling unwanted, and the greatest evil was the lack of love and charity and the terrible indifference towards one's neighbour. 'Love begins at home,' she said. 'Families that pray together, stay together. Unless you stay together, you cannot love one another, and unless you love one another, you cannot love anyone else.' She said these words with earnestness. The break-up of the family in the West was of the greatest concern to her. 'True love hurts,' she said. 'It must be painful to love someone; you might have to die for them.'

She thought deeply on issues like sin. 'Sin is nothing but slavery. When I choose evil, I sin. It's where my will comes in. When I seek something for myself at the cost of everything else, I deliberately choose sin. Very often in a desire to get something there's greed, there's jealousy, there's destruction. We cannot see God then. It is an obstacle . . . To be clean of heart means obedience, that complete freedom.'

Mother Teresa was one of the busiest women in the world but came across as one of the most relaxed. And this attitude came from a complete trust in God. She believed in 'accepting whatever He sends you and giving Him whatever He takes from you'. The latter could include a loved one.

She did not worry. 'It is not my business to think about myself,' she said. 'It is my business to think about God. It is for God to think about me.' This freedom from self made it possible for her and the nuns she trained to make herculean demands on their frail bodies. They all woke up between 4 and 4.30 a.m., meditated and prayed for half an hour, attended Mass each day, washed, cleaned, cooked and then were out on the streets or at their jobs at 7 a.m. It was a gruelling schedule.

'I could not do for a day what I am doing,' said Mother, 'without attending Mass and having this time of contemplation and prayer. Our work is the fruit of our prayer. For twenty-four hours as we work, we are teaching Christ. The more we receive in silent prayer, the more we can give in our active life.'

'Love to pray,' she said, 'feel often during the day the

need for prayer, take the trouble to pray. Prayer enlarges the heart. Work doesn't stop prayer and prayer doesn't stop work.' She had set times for morning and evening prayers. Throughout the day she was often too busy but always had time for short prayers like, 'I love You, God, I trust You, I believe in You, I need You now.' She conditioned her mind and drew strength through these brief prayers.

From time to time she felt the need to withdraw herself, and in those quiet moments with God she recharged her spirit.

What classed Mother Teresa above some contemplatives was her motivation. 'We must become holy not because we want to feel holy, but because Christ must be able to live His life fully in us.' The two commandments of Christ were, 'Love the Lord thy God and love thy neighbour as thyself.'

How many of us stop at the first commandment because we seek holiness for ourselves? Even our good actions are often motivated by self-interest. Mother Teresa broke out of that box of spiritual solace. She made you measure your life against hers, your selfishness with her sacrifice; your over-busyness with her sense of peace and calm in the midst of her merciless schedule. A British VIP came in a three-piece suit to visit her and saw her work. When he left and was about to step into the grand limousine of the British High Commission, he said to his companion, 'This suit burns me up.' She had the unconscious gift of making us relate our lives to hers. And in that process people changed. A non-practising Christian journalist, Desmond Doig, wrote a fine biography of her. He was not the same afterwards. Doig concluded, 'She taught me to see, not merely to look; to appreciate, not merely to understand.'

One day Fr. Le Joly S.J., her long time co-worker,

ventured to ask, 'May I write about you and your Sisters?'* He thought she would be cool to his proposal as much had been written about her. But she answered immediately, 'Father, do it. Tell them we are not here for the work, we are here for Jesus. We are religious, not social workers, not nurses, not teachers, we are religious sisters. All we do, our prayer, our work, our suffering is for Jesus . . . He gives me strength. I love Him in the poor and the poor in Him. Without Jesus our life would be meaningless, incomprehensible . . .' She thumped her fist on the table and summed up, 'Father, tell them: We do it for Jesus.' Fr. Le Joly left the house happy. He had the title for his next book, *We do it for Jesus*.

'Silence,' she says, 'is the beautiful fruit of prayer. We must learn not only the silence of the mouth but also the silence of the heart, of the eyes, of the ears and of the mind, which I call the five silences. Say it and memorize it on your five fingers.'

When I asked her, 'Do you think your work will continue after you?'

'Oh yes,' she replied with an emphatic turn of the head, 'if He finds someone even more helpless than me, He will still continue. God has been just wonderful.'

Postscript:

In August 1996 Mother Teresa was critically ill in Calcutta. School-children in India, and individuals all over the world prayed for her. Two days before her eighty-sixth birthday, after a night of suffering, she whispered,

---

* From *The Joy in Loving—A Guide to Daily Living with Mother Teresa*—Compiled by Jaya Chaliha and Edward Le Joly.

> I don't know what God is doing,
> He knows.
> We do not understand
> But one thing I'm sure
> He doesn't make a mistake.

Her first disciple, Sister Agnes, who was herself seriously ill at that time, prayed that Mother Teresa survive a while longer. Mother Teresa made a miraculous recovery. It was Sister Agnes who passed away. In the year to follow, 1997, Mother Teresa went to Rome, to her Homes in the US and returned in July 1997. A few months later, on 5 September 1997, at Mother's House in Calcutta, she passed away.

In an unprecedented homage, Mother Teresa was given a State funeral. Princes, Heads of State, and people whom she had brought new life to, came from all over the world to pay homage to this daughter of a simple Albanian peasant.

M.S. Subbulakshmi

Any raga has the purpose of directing the minds of the listeners towards God and his manifestations.

'Who am I, a mere prime minister, before the Queen of Song!' said Jawaharlal Nehru after a performance by M.S. Subbulakshmi.

To hear M.S. Subbulakshmi sing is an ennobling experience. To meet her is a humbling one. Few have greater claims to be proud; yet, for all her attainments, she is a model of humility. There is a secret about this 'enchanting singer with an enchanting voice', as Sarojini Naidu called her. Wherein does her secret lie?

At over eighty years of age she remains the most renowned artist of India. As a mark of this, the Bharat Ratna, the nation's highest honour, has been bestowed on her. She started her singing career at the age of eighteen when she sang in the Madras Music Academy. Experienced singers were quick to acknowledge her talent. Six years later, in 1940, she married T. Sadasivam. Soon after she acted in her sole film, *Mira*. Through that film, it is said, she 'aroused the dormant spirituality of millions in south and north India'.

Since then, Subbulakshmi has given concert recitals throughout the length and breadth of India, from coast to coast in America, in South-East Asia, and in the capitals of

Illustration by Manjula Padmanabhan

Europe. She has sung at the Edinburgh Festival in 1963 and at the UN in 1966.

In 1974, she was given the Ramon Magsaysay Award for Public Service. The citation spoke of her as a 'spiritual singer to many millions in India' whose exalted rendering of devotional songs has supported numerous public causes in the country for four decades.

'MS', as she is called, has raised crores of rupees for charities. Her husband once told me that the only money she accepted for herself was Rs 20,000 for her role in *Mira*. This she handed over to him and with it he bought Kalki Gardens which became their home and seat of the magazine *Kalki* that enthralled thousands for four decades. 'All that she has with her now,' Sadasivam had confided softly to me, 'is the jewellery she brought with her when she married me.'

Thanks to my colleague, Rajmohan Gandhi, a close family friend of theirs, I too was invited to stay at the Sadasivams' Kalki home in 1966. It was an old home with large rooms and a spacious veranda. Often one heard the veena being played as MS had time earmarked for practice. She owes her interest in music to her mother who was a distinguished veena player. At a young age, she accompanied her mother.

I got to know MS and her husband better in February 1978 when she came to Panchgani after a recital in Pune. Even in the leisure and quiet of that place, her serenity stood out. Over meals, she spoke little. When questioned, she often looked at her husband with a smile and the witty Sadasivam was never short of words. As they were leaving, someone asked her to sign in the Visitor's Book. The celebrity said, 'My husband should sign first.' 'I owe all to my husband,' she added. 'By his loving care, he is my parent; by his unerring guidance, he is my preceptor.'

Sadasivam was also among her most ardent admirers. It has always been an experience to hear MS give a concert but it was a double treat to sit in the second row behind her husband! He enjoyed rapturously every moment of the recital, and occasionally signalled to his daughter, Radha, seated next to MS, if an impromptu number or encore was to be given.

When Subbulakshmi makes her debut on the dais, she does it reverently. She is no prima donna. She does not want to attract attention to herself. She settles down with her daughter and her accompanists as they take time to tune their instruments.

Then the voice that has thrilled millions is heard. First you drink in the appealing timbre of her voice, then you marvel at her technical virtuosity. Thereafter, you get absorbed emotionally and as the programme continues, you feel that the pettiness and the struggle of life around you is being lifted up and you are on another plane. In her devotion and charm she has carried you nearer to her Creator—and yours.

MS once explained, 'Bhakti is nothing but the devotion that we show to the divinity that resides within us. Once we regard the divinity within us with devotional fervour, we are bound to develop the same affection towards everything outside. The reason is that the same divine truth runs through all things. When the devotee has attained this state, service to the world becomes his creed. Tyagaraja has given a convincing illustration of this truth in his composition, *Sukhi Evaro*. He lays down that the man who sings in praise of God is he who upholds truth, who is always at the service of humanity, to whom all gods and goddesses are the same and who sings with an impeccable voice. From this we understand that truth, service and impartiality should go hand in hand with a sweet voice. The poet Bharati says, "If there is radiance in the heart, there will be radiance in the voice." A pure mind and a sweet voice cannot be separated from each other.'

C.V. Narasimhan, former deputy secretary-general of the UN, who has known MS for over forty years, says, 'To understand her as a musician, one has to know her as a person. The qualities of humility, simplicity and dedication that mark her personal life, are abundantly reflected in her music. I believe that the key to great music is humility to the point of self-effacement. The singer then becomes a pure vehicle, an interpreter rather than a virtuoso showing off his own talents.'

She enjoys being with her accompanists and keeps time with their instruments, tapping her hand. She looks affectionately at them as their fingers flutter and the drummers conduct a lively dialogue with each other. Because she is not self-centred, she has all the time for other people and interest in them.

Her life is of one piece. As she is on stage, so she is off it. Her accompanist, Vinayakram, told me of the love he gets from MS and her husband. 'Because they give sacrificially,' he said, 'I like to work with them.'

'Any raga,' says MS, 'has the purpose of directing the minds of the listeners towards God and his manifestations.' Devotion inspires her singing. 'Bhakti,' she says, 'should go hand in hand with a virtuous mind. Those who wish to take to the fine art of music must be good people. It may not be easy to be a good person. There is, however, a great advantage. There is no time bar to becoming good. There is no question of becoming a doctor, an engineer or a lawyer after a certain age. But there is no age limit for anyone to become a good person. In the mind of a good person bhakti is an instinctive growth. God Himself makes His home in such a mind.'

In her presidential address to the Madras Music Academy in 1968, she observed, 'Students of music should devote their attention to the acquisition of purity in voice and *sruti*. To achieve this, it is essential that they should practise voice culture assiduously. One should not be content with possessing a sweet voice; in the manner in which land is ploughed to yield a good crop, the voice should be cultivated in order to get the best out of it. The voice should be made to traverse the three octaves with felicity, curbing the tendency to branch into a falsetto. Knowledge of the exact position of *swaras* is most important. This cannot be learnt from notation or written tests. If learnt in that way, it will remain only as theoretical knowledge and will not blossom into the art of music. The manner in which the *swaras* are woven into the various ragas in our Karnatic music can be best studied by playing them on the veena.'

The veena, which can be heard in the sanctum sanctorum of a temple, was not only her mother's instrument. MS is accomplished at playing it herself. Everyone, she believes, should study music as they study history or geography or arithmetic, for we live in a restless world and a world of violence.

The violinist, Yehudi Menhuin, once said, if peace and good conduct are to prevail in the present-day world, it is essential that the appreciation of music grows in a big way. 'Let there be less of speaking,' said Menhuin, 'and more of music; and periods of silence when the music also has to stop.'

MS echoes these words.

M.S. Swaminathan

People are poor because they have no knowledge or skills. Give them that and they lift themselves from degradation to an honourable existence.

A young Indian scientist was pleading with senior bureaucrats of the agriculture ministry for a grant of Rs 50,000 for organizing 100 demonstrations of new wheat varieties in the fields of small farmers. He said he had experimented with the Mexican variety of dwarf wheat which agriculturist and later Nobel Prize winner Norman Borlaug had experimented with in Mexico. The wheat was developed at the Agriculture Institute at Pusa and he wanted to try it out in the field with farmers. The bureaucrats dissuaded him. 'The Indian farmer is conservative. He won't accept new techniques.' 'It is a waste of money.' Undeterred, the young man went up to C. Subramaniam, minister for food and agriculture, and pleaded, 'Let the farmer decide what is acceptable or not.' The minister agreed.

The Indian farmer eagerly tried it and avidly propagated it. It is he who took it forward. Swaminathan and his colleagues did a superb job ensuring that the new wheat variety reached every nook and corner of India.

After the Bihar famine of 1966, Western experts like Paul Ehrlich and the Paddock brothers predicted mass scale

Illustration by Gautam Roy

starvation in India in the 1970s. Instead, a miracle happened. India's wheat production, which stood at 12 million tonnes in 1967, jumped to 20 million tonnes in two years; 24 million tonnes by 1974-75; 44 million tonnes by 1984-85; and 72 million tonnes by 1994-95.

In his book, *A Century of Hope*, Dr Swaminathan looked at the next century. He writes,

> It is clear that if children are to be born for happiness in the coming millennium, nature, humanity and technology must work in harmony . . . We need a paradigm shift in our approach to technology development. Natural resource management concerns must be integrated in genetic improvement methodologies. Sir Francis Bacon once said, 'It would be an unsound fancy to expect that things which have never yet been done can be done except by methods which have never been tried.'

Dr Swaminathan is searching for and applying these new methods.

In the late 1960s, it was a team of Indian agricultural scientists, officials and farmers who brought about the miracle of the Green Revolution, but the leadership and the thrust was provided by Swaminathan. Javier Perez de Cuellar, UN secretary-general, said: 'Dr Swaminathan is a living legend. His contribution to agricultural science has made an indelible mark on food production in India and elsewhere in the developing world. By any standards he will go down in history as a world scientist of rare distinction.'

In actual fact, the man who first developed a dwarf wheat using material from Japan was Dr Orville Vogel in

Washington, but it was Dr Borlaug who first developed semi-dwarf wheat varieties, based on the Japanese dwarfing gene.

Dr Borlaug won the Nobel Prize for his pioneering work in 1970. He credited Dr Swaminathan for recognizing the potential value of the dwarfing genes, saying, 'The green revolution has been a team effort and much of the credit for its spectacular development must go to the Indian officials, organizations, scientists and farmers. However, to you, Dr Swaminathan, a great deal of credit must go for first recognizing the potential value of the Mexican dwarf wheat. Had this not occurred, it is possible that there would not have been a green revolution in Asia.'

Thirty years later, Dr Swaminathan (called MS by friends) is as involved with his work as ever. Now, he says, we need an 'evergreen revolution' with sustainable farming that is kind to the land, to water resources and the crops. Development, he says, is needed, 'but technology must harmonize with the environment. It is possible to have both technology and care for the environment.' This approach to development is called ecotechnology—a concept he has advanced. He now occupies the UNESCO chair in ecotechnology and adjoining his foundation stands the J.R.D. Tata Centre for Ecotechnology.

We talked about his life while relaxing in a hotel in Chennai. The man who carries the tongue-twisting name Moncompu (village name) Sambasivan (father's name) Swaminathan (his given name) was born in Kumbakonam in Tamil Nadu in 1925 in the family of a surgeon. His father came from Kerala and settled in Kumbakonam, a town then notorious for filariasis.

'The principles of self-reliance, love towards all and community effort were inculcated in me during the first ten years of my life. I learnt from my father that the word "impossible" exists mainly in our minds and that given the requisite will and effort, great tasks can be accomplished,' Swaminathan said.

Swaminathan recalls how his father, a follower of Mahatma Gandhi, took the lead in their area in 'burning his foreign clothes', a symbolic act advocated by the Mahatma in support of the swadeshi movement which emphasized the use of Indian rather than foreign-made clothes; and handloom in preference to mill-spun cloth. The purpose of swadeshi was to free India from dependence on foreign imports and to protect village industry. His father also led in opening the temples to 'untouchables'. The higher caste boycotted Swaminathan's father for his courageous stand. His father spearheaded the campaign for eradicating filariasis in Kumbakonam, an area long infected with the dread disease. The sense of service to one's fellowmen was thus ingrained in Swaminathan early in life.

After his father's death, when he was eleven, young Swaminathan was looked after by his uncle, M.K. Narayanaswami, a radiologist. Swaminathan attended the local high school and later the Catholic Little Flower High School in Kumbakonam, from which he passed out when he was fifteen. He went on to get his Bachelor of Science degree in zoology from the University of Travancore (now Kerala University) in 1944. At that point, he decided to take up the study of agriculture.

When I asked him about the deciding factor which made him take up agricultural research—when he was also fond of zoology—he replied, 'The Bengal famine of 1943.' The suffering and deaths left a deep impression on him.

'Did any book influence you profoundly?' I asked him.

'Yes. It was by an ICS official, F.L. Brayne, called *Socrates in an Indian Village*. Though a Britisher, he comprehended what Gandhi was trying to do for our villages—sanitation, latrines, organic farming.' Swaminathan's desire to help the poor received a sense of direction from this book.

Swaminathan had spent his holidays in the 'rice bowls' of Kerala and Tamil Nadu and had been struck by the paucity of the grain yield and the poverty of farmers. In contrast, he noticed that plantation crops—coffee, rubber, tea—grew well in the same soil and conditions. His observations awakened his interest in agricultural problems and he read widely, discovering that crop yields in India were very low compared to other countries. 'The interaction between heredity and environment fascinated me,' Swaminathan later said, 'hence, in 1944, I decided to take to agricultural education, and since then I have developed what my wife, Mina, says is a "single track mind", concerned with problems of improving agricultural productivity and agrarian prosperity.'

He received a Bachelor of Science degree in agriculture from the University of Madras in 1947 and did postgraduate work at the Indian Agricultural Research Institute (IARI), from which he received an associate diploma (with high distinction) in cytogenetics two years later. Swaminathan passed the Indian Administrative Services examination and was offered a post in the Indian Police Service. At the same time he was informed about his being the recipient of a UNESCO fellowship to study abroad. Choosing to pursue his studies from 1949 to 1950, he was a UNESCO Fellow[*] in the Institute of Genetics at the Agricultural University of

---

[*] Almost fifty years later, he was the first recipient of the UNESCO Gandhi Gold Medal for his work on biodiversity in India's villages.

Wageningen in the Netherlands. From there, he proceeded to Cambridge, where he received a Doctorate of Philosophy in 1952 for his thesis, 'Species Differentiation and Nature of Polyploidy in Tuber-Bearing Solanum Species.' It presented an 'entirely fresh concept of the relationships within the tuber-bearing Solanums (potatoes)'.

To broaden his experience before returning home, he accepted an appointment as research associate in genetics at the University of Wisconsin in the US, from November 1952 to January 1954. There he continued his work on the potato.

He soon applied his knowledge of potato genetic research to other crops. He received an attractive offer to continue research in the US but declined politely. 'I came to equip myself, not work in a foreign country,' he said.

On his return, he worked at the Indian Agricultural Research Institute and rose to be its director twelve years later. Scores of agricultural scientists qualified during his tenure and they still treat him respectfully as their 'guru'.

From 1972 to 1979 he worked with the Indian Council of Agricultural Research (ICAR) as its director-general. In 1979, when Morarji Desai was prime minister, he summoned Swaminathan and asked him to become secretary, ministry of agriculture. Till then this post had always been occupied by IAS personnel. Surprised, he asked Morarji why he was chosen. 'Because I want an agricultural secretary to know agriculture,' Morarji replied.

In 1980, when Indira Gandhi came to power, she appointed Swaminathan to the Planning Commission. During the Janata rule earlier, when Indira Gandhi was in political wilderness from 1977 to 1980, she would often go to see Vinoba Bhave at Wardha for solace and comfort.

When Indira Gandhi unexpectedly came to power again

and went to see Vinoba, he handed her a slip, 'Make Wardha Jilla into a Gandhi Jilla.' Intrigued, Indira recounted this incident to Swaminathan as she appointed him to the Planning Commission. Vinoba could have meant an area where nobody lived below the poverty line. Swaminathan also presided over Committees for the Eradication of Leprosy and Blindness. But Planning bored him. He was a man of action. In 1981, the chairman of the prestigious International Rice Research Institute of the Philippines came to Delhi and requested Swaminathan to become its director-general. When Swaminathan mentioned the offer to P.C. Alexander, then secretary to Mrs Gandhi, he replied, 'She'll never let you go.' Swaminathan met the prime minister.

'You are indispensable,' she said.

'Because you say so, I'm indispensable, I think I should go, since I believe one must leave when one is wanted.'

Looking back, Swaminathan says, 'Sometimes, words come to us of this nature which make the difference.'

The prime minister thought again. To his surprise, she said slowly, 'Yes, you must leave when you are (still) wanted.'

She repeated sadly but wisely, 'You must leave when you are wanted. You have my blessings.'

After six challenging rich years in the Philippines, Swaminathan returned to India and was awarded the first World Food Prize in 1987 of $2,00,000. Other honours followed. In 1991 he received the Tyler Prize (for environment, shared), $1,50,000; in 1992, the Honda Award for Ecotechnology, $1,50,000; in 1994, the UNEP's Sasakawa Award, $1,25,000; in 1996, the Blue Planet Award (to his foundation), $5,00,000; and in 1999, the Volvo Environment Prize, $1,75,000.

Earlier, he had received the Ramon Magsaysay Award for

Community Leadership (1972); the first award of the International Association of Women in Development (1984); and the Albert Einstein World Science Award (1986).

With his World Food Prize he started the M.S. Swaminathan Research Foundation in Chennai in 1989. Swaminathan's third stage of life began. The purpose of the M.S. Swaminathan Research Foundation is spelt out by him. Swaminathan is a visionary in his thinking and a missionary in his dedication to fulfil his ideas.

'The poor are poor,' says Swaminathan, 'because they have no knowledge or skills. Give them that and you empower them. The only way to abolish poverty is to build the assets of the poor and they will lift themselves from degradation to an honourable existence.' The work of his foundation, with its state-of-the-art research facilities, is implemented in the field by the J.R.D. Tata Centre for Ecotechnology, equipped substantially by funding from the Tata Trusts.

Through the centre's work, Swaminathan has seen downtrodden people who were eking out a miserable existence transform their lives. I asked him from where he found his passion to continue this work. 'Working for the poor gives you inner strength. They are blossoms in the dust but they can become personalities with self-confidence, self-esteem,' he replied.

His dedicated group of scientists are also fieldworkers. When they go to a village, they first survey the prospects. If there is a derelict pond, they improve it and offer facilities for aquaculture. Wherever big pipes are found abandoned in a village, they are sealed and converted into receptacles for cultivating ornamental fish. When women in a village accomplished this, the foundation found the market to export the fish to Singapore. The women now earn Rs 1,000 to Rs 1,200 per month. In dry areas of Tamil Nadu, millet and pulses were introduced and farmers found a fair living.

Swaminathan who has been heaped with laurels, awards and forty doctorates from universities round the world, is a soft-spoken man of arresting humility and inexhaustible energy. At seventy-four, his travels are frequent and often to far-flung places. He has a kind heart and hates to say 'No' to invitations that descend on him. Even so, his discipline and efficiency is such that his foundation and he constantly notch up achievements to their credit. His spirit of dedication attracts young people to work with him.

Prof. V.N. Chopra, who was director-general of the Indian Council of Agricultural Research, says that when he was a pupil of Prof. Swaminathan, students had to do fieldwork. A certain cotton seed had to be planted at 5.30 a.m. When the boys went to the field, Swaminathan was already there—they planted the seeds and he levelled the earth.

Perhaps the driving force in Swaminathan's life is his concern for the hungry, the poor and the deprived women. He noted women are usually the main producers of food in most Asian countries and yet they are the least fed. He is deeply concerned about the neglect of nutrition for pregnant women and the consequent birth of weak babies. He calls it 'the cruellest act'. One-third of our children are undernourished and underweight. He is concerned about a 'hidden hunger' that comes from poverty in the midst of availability of food. He rejoices when using simple methods, his foundation teaches women to grow high-paid variety of crops and cultivate ornamental fish or prawn. He has broadened his interests and expertise for the protection of mangroves (India has 60 per cent of the world's variety), and to preserve the unique underwater life of the Gulf of Mannar, a world heritage site.

His foundation building is simply designed with a garden that represents the five elements of nature.

Swaminathan lives in a modest house in Chennai with his wife who is the daughter of a well-known ICS official, Mr Boothalingam. Mina qualified with a tripos in economics and mathematics at Cambridge, but was more interested in working for people than with figures. She went on to specialize in pre-primary education. She felt she needed to awaken the thinking of people—about themselves, their attitudes, their lives. 'Outer change begins with inner change,' she says. She feels that plays can spark off people's imagination and the ability to look inward. Her work of pre-primary education also involves the staging of plays to stimulate people mentally. Their three daughters have inherited their parents' passion to work for social good through different disciplines.

When asked if he ever felt destiny had played a part in his success, Swaminathan replies that the factors that took him forward are 'hard work, some inspiration, luck, destiny'. To these, he adds, 'grace'. He believes, though he is too shy to spell it out, that the divine has blessed his efforts and has made him an instrument of His grace.

The amazing quality about Swaminathan is that over the years, his interests, expertise and commitment to subjects dear to him have grown and his sympathies have widened. From food production, he has moved to nutrition security. From agricultural development, he has graduated to human development. From an interest in environment, to a concern for the well-being of the malnourished child and the neglected pregnant woman. And to his interests he brings to bear his well-honed scientific mind, which can zero in and stay on a particular subject and search out an intelligent way to solve a problem.

There are 140 good government schemes for the poor, but they don't reach them, Swaminathan observes. He now wants to use the newly acquired powers of the Panchayati Raj and modern information technology for the upliftment of the people and to empower the weak.

Of all the letters he has received announcing various awards, perhaps no one has been worded as well as that from the chairman of the Roosevelt Institute. Informing Swaminathan of being chosen for the Franklin D. Roosevelt Four Freedoms Medal in 2000, the letter says,

> Your extraordinary work as an agricultural scientist, leading the 'green revolution' and bringing hope to the peoples of the developing nations so that the age-old scourge of famine and hunger can be ended, has been particularly noted. You have taught nations how to be self-sufficient in their need for food just as you have taught farmers how to develop and enhance the productivity of their land. Your brilliant leadership has established a goal for the new millennium—a hunger-free world, an international structure of co-operation among nations, a determination to use the miraculous technology of our times to help those in need. Your dynamism and compassion have given new meaning to Franklin Delano Roosevelt's commitment to a better world where all nations will understand and strive for Freedom from Want.

Swaminathan's work will never be over for the needs of humanity will never end. Deep in our hearts most of us yearn for our lives to be useful, to wipe a few tears from some eyes. We have to be satisfied with that. The work of Swaminathan and his colleagues is reaching out to more people and on a much larger scale. Smiling faces are his greatest reward—greater than any award can be.

Nani Palkhivala

Surely something is basically wrong with our economic philosophy and political ideology if Indians are able to enrich foreign countries but are not allowed to solve the problem of poverty at home.

In the cool of an early March evening in the mid-sixties, thousands had gathered on the spacious East Lawns of Bombay's Cricket Club of India to hear Nani Palkhivala speak on the Budget. Half an hour before the meeting, a swelling crowd had occupied strategic position. Among them were Parsis who belonged to Nani's tiny community and did not appear to be the kind who had much to worry about regarding the Budget. Nonetheless, they turned up in full strength to hear *apro* Nani (our Nani). There are usually two or three personalities in a generation to whom the Parsis attach the fond Gujarati prefix *apro*. In the old days, Queen Victoria was *apri* Rani. Dadabhoy Naoroji and Jamsetji Tata are still called *apro*.

There, before an urban audience, Nani started speaking. 'Every Budget,' he said, 'contains a cartload of figures in black and white—but the stark figures represent the myriad lights and shades of India's life, the contrasting tones of poverty and wealth, and of bread so dear and flesh and blood so cheap, the deep tints of adventure and enterprise and man's ageless struggle for a brighter morn.'

He reeled off facts, figures and statistics—decimal points and all—without any notes. He punctuated his oration with quotations from Shakespeare, Lord Acton, Jawaharlal Nehru and C. Rajagopalachari. The audience cheered him as he assailed the 'boneless wonders' and the 'bumbling bureaucrats' of Delhi. At the end of the oration of *apro* Nani, his admirers braced themselves and strode out—fortified to fight another day. No non-political figure in India could draw people the way Nani did from the 1960s to the 1990s. In later years, a good section of the Brabourne Stadium and its lawns were filled with up to 1,00,000 people who were there to hear him speak.

Nani Palkhivala is absolutely sure he is what he is only because of his parents' influence. 'My father, Ardeshir, taught me compassion and kindness for the less privileged,' Palkhivala said to an interviewer, his eyes moist with tears.

He wiped his eyes and continued with a smile, 'I remember, I was not more than two years old. I was about to help myself to a bowl of almonds when my father reminded me of the poor orphan who lived next door. I was so moved by his words that I immediately handed over the entire bowl to the boy. That incident has made a deep impression on me ever since.'

Constitutional lawyer, tax expert, economic developer, diplomat, author, Nani Palkhivala has adorned all that he has touched in life. He was born on 16 January 1920, in the home of a small businessman. Money was short in the family, but Nani's hopes were high. As a young boy he devoured books. Samuel Smiles' book, *Self-Help*, inspired him. From Tutorial High School he went to St. Xavier's College, Bombay. By the time he was sixteen, he started earning by

Illustration by Manjula Padmanabhan

giving tuitions. At college he studied English literature and won the Chancellor's Medal in his MA.

From 1943 to 1946 Nani read law, securing a First Class First at the LL.B and Advocate examinations. He was soon appointed professor at the Bombay Law College and was honoured with the Tagore Professorship of Law at Calcutta University. He first won distinction by producing an authoritative work on income tax law, in association with his senior, Sir Jamshedji Kanga, in whose chambers he started his career. 'Apart from the nitty-gritty which I picked up from him, he taught me the virtue of modesty.'

The flame of achievement burned in him. He fought case after case of national importance. His victories at the Supreme Court were impressive. He fought and won the Bank Nationalization Case. In 1971, due to his advocacy, the Supreme Court struck down the government's order to take away the privy purses of princes by unconstitutional methods. He argued the famous Fundamental Rights Case (1973), heard by thirteen judges of the Supreme Court over a period of five months, in which the Supreme Court ruled that Parliament cannot so amend the Constitution as to alter or destroy its basic structure.

Nani successfully argued for the Fundamental Rights of Minorities to administer educational and religious institutions of their choice, and to choose the language in which education should be imparted.

Princes as well as impoverished priests felt confident that they could count on his sympathies. He fought most cases of public importance without charging any fees. Although he was for many years a vociferous critic of Congress governments, a succession of its law ministers invariably honoured him by giving him briefs for India at international tribunals, like the International Court at the Hague.

Nani brought to bear upon complicated legal issues his lucid interpretation, but with it came a spaciousness of mind and a generosity of spirit which lifted the issues way beyond legal niceties. For example, when there were reports that the Nobel Prize of Mother Teresa may be subject to taxation by the Law Ministry, he floored the bureaucrats not only on the issue of law but also on the question of their meanness. Promptly, the bureaucrats backtracked.

At one time as the country's foremost practising lawyer Nani netted an enormous income despite forgoing his fees in many cases. After fifteen years at the Bar, Nani came to the conclusion that he would rather participate in the nation's economic development than defend litigants which thousands of other lawyers could do as well. He came to Tatas as a legal adviser, got more and more involved in industrial development and in the late 1970s became the deputy chairman of two of India's largest companies—Tata Steel and Telco. J.R.D. Tata gave him special permission to attend to his legal practice, which he selectively did for cases of national importance and for private consultations. For several years, Nani was chairman of ACC, the mega cement combine. In his annual chairman's statements, Nani, in a few bold strokes, brilliantly highlighted the state of the economy.

What was it like to work with him on an industrial board? Kamaljit Singh, who headed the Indian Oil Corporation and later joined ACC as managing director, listed among Nani's qualities 'the ability to grasp a problem quickly, and the ability to take quick decisions. In my forty years in the industry, I have never encountered an individual who combines the qualities of integrity, compassion and concern for human relations with the ability to take firm and even unpleasant decisions to the same extent as Palkhivala'.

Opportunities in business provide Nani the space to exercise those qualities of the heart that go way beyond the intellectual gymnastics that law often demands. And to complete the picture, Nani supports movements that enrich the spirit of man, be it of Sri Aurobindo's or Satya Sai Baba's. For him, life has always been larger than law, business or politics. His knowledge on matters outside the legal field is remarkable. In his book, *India's Heritage*, he reveals his profound knowledge of the Vedas. Associated with big business, Nani tries to inject into its policies his sense of 'old values and sincerity of purpose', as a colleague puts it. He has not been interested in the controversy over public and private sector. 'There are only two sectors,' he says, 'the efficient and the inefficient.'

Though a critic of Prime Minister Indira Gandhi, Nani accepted her election appeal brief in the Supreme Court because he felt she had a good case and that every litigant was entitled to his or her choice of a lawyer. On 24 June 1975, Nani obtained an interim judgement permitting Mrs Gandhi to remain prime minister but not to vote in Parliament. He assured Mrs Gandhi she had nothing to fear and was confident of winning her case. Even so, on the midnight of 25-26 June, she clamped down the Emergency. Within hours, Nani returned Mrs Gandhi's brief, 'consistent with my lifelong convictions and the values I cherish', he told me.

Through most of the Emergency, Nani was silent but in December 1975, at the height of the Emergency, when the government sought to compel the Supreme Court to review its decision in the Fundamental Rights Case, Nani took up the case and convinced the Supreme Court that such a review was unnecessary. Due to the strict censorship, his victory was little publicized.

When the Janata Government came to power in 1977, Foreign Minister Atal Behari Vajpayee asked him to be the US ambassador. Nani replied he would like to serve in India. Then Prime Minister Morarji Desai called him, and when Nani repeated this request to him, Morarji in his usual blunt manner said, 'It is not for you to decide.' Nani accepted on condition that he would return within eighteen months. He kept his lien on his post at Bombay House, the Tata headquarters. In eighteen months, he criss-crossed America and introduced India to the American public, specially the universities, as no previous ambassador had done.

The president of the 20,000-strong Associations of Indians in America, commenting on Nani's term as ambassador said, 'For the first time we got a feeling that Indians were welcome at the embassy and today we can get our passport in twenty-four hours and a visa in a couple of hours.'

For Nani himself, the American experience was an eye-opener. 'All over the United States—from the Boeing workshop in Seattle to the Texas Instruments in Dallas, to the Institute of Technology at Massachusetts—Indian talent is employed and the men in charge expressed to me their gratitude to India for giving them such remarkable human resources. Surely something is basically wrong with our economic philosophy and political ideology if Indians are able to enrich foreign countries but are not allowed to solve the problem of poverty at home.'

He brought back from the US a list of highly qualified Indian scientists willing to assist in India but, alas, the bureaucracy did not move fast enough to take advantage of their offer.

Nani had told the government that he would go as

ambassador only for eighteen months. When his tenure was over, he returned to India because his heart was in his own country. 'There is so much to do here,' he said. Incidentally, immediately on his arrival, the Janata Government fell, and in the ensuing confusion, many hoped that Nani would enter public life. He declined, and disappointed many who had pinned their hopes on him. He said, 'Yes, sometimes one does feel inadequate.' What would have happened had he taken the political plunge? It is a sad commentary that no political party acceptable to him nominated him even to the Upper House of Parliament. Nani chose to vigorously support men of integrity who were standing for Parliament in 1980 and who, he felt, would help to shape the India of his dreams.

I have seen Nani full of hope and promise in the late 1970s—a man who believed India could be shaped according to his dreams. I have met Nani in the late 1980s and early 1990s. The hopes of yesteryear have dimmed and he tends to be quite negative about the country.

He yearns to work with men who would harness the immense economic potential of this land—men who would employ the 40 million idle hands in productive work. He is impatient with laws and rules that stunt our industry and our nation.

A gentleman in the true sense, I've noted during car rides that he speaks in the same tone to his driver as he would to a cabinet minister.

I once accompanied him to Dr Ambedkar Law College in Bombay, where students crowded into a lecture hall and waited with eager faces as he entered to address them. 'One thing I would recommend,' Nani told them, 'is poverty in young age. It makes you appreciate human values—like love at home.'

If Nani is asked how he graduated from literature to law, from law to taxation, from taxation to economics, he looks lost. 'There is nothing conscious about it. No human being can plan these things. What are we puny mortals? I believe in a Higher Force.'

'Do you believe in a personal God?' I asked him.

'No, but I do believe in a divine force,' he replied.

Distinguished men who have influenced him are: Sir Jamshedji Kanga, Rajaji, and later Jayaprakash Narayan, but if you are looking for the secret of his success, you have to look elsewhere.

He has a sound value system. 'To me, money is only a means to an end. And that end is doing good to others.' To Nani, the most important thing for a person—as for a nation—is productive use of time and energy. And Nani, as long as his health permitted him to do so, endeavoured to fill every moment of his life productively, whether he was handling a legal case, an industry meeting or an interview. He always seemed in a hurry, often quite restless in a private interview, but supremely composed while addressing a gathering of as many as 10,000 people. This restlessness tended to make it difficult for the other person to have a deeper dialogue with him. His strength—the use of time—tended to be his weakness too.

I first saw Nani in 1945 as he strode across the quadrangle of St. Xavier's College. He had a spring in his step and a shock of unruly, kinky hair. When I first met him in 1963, he had great hopes about India, but as decades passed and he saw the erosion of public institutions and the conduct of our public figures, he despaired about the future of the country.

Perhaps no single lawyer since Independence has fought

as many significant court cases as Nani. Over lunch in 1998, I asked him the secret of his success. He thought for a moment and replied modestly, 'I always want to do my best.' His wife, Nergish, chipped in, 'Even when young people like myself liked to fool around (in college), Nani was very hard working.' They had met at St. Xavier's College.

Years earlier, J.R.D. Tata had expressed amazement at Nani's collection of quotations and the meticulous way he had filed them. I felt it may be educative to see what Nani had done, so I asked him about it. I thought it would be a few volumes of handwritten quotations, subjectwise or indexed. Instead, there were three cupboards full, each cupboard about eight feet by two or three feet, where files were arranged in close proximity under different subjects. Quotations were typed. One file had select quotations by US Presidents, all handpicked by Nani. He finds it difficult to write by hand as he has writer's cramp. In all his exams, he had a writer. It must have been difficult for him to even note down the quotations. He advises young people to read a good book every morning at the start of day. His index system for quotations was remarkable. I wondered how a man, who has had such a busy life, could ever find the time for this work. Apart from hard work it shows the discipline of the man. It was a lifetime's work and when I asked him, 'Should it not be published?' he gently indicated that he was not interested 'at the end of my life'. He was then eighty. His wife, extremely intelligent and skilled in the use of the English language, was a student of higher mathematics.

Nani has also produced two very fine books of his speeches and occasional writings. The first, *We the People*, was a best-seller and the second, *We the Nation*, did equally well. The dedication of *We the People* sums up his thinking:

TO MY COUNTRYMEN
who gave unto themselves the Constitution
but not the ability to keep it,

who inherited a resplendent heritage
but not the wisdom to cherish it,

who suffer and endure in patience
without the perception of their potential.

I once asked him what he enjoyed the most in his many splendoured life—his court cases, his speeches or other activities like business. Without hesitation, he replied, 'Court cases.' I inquired which was the most challenging. Again, without hesitation, he replied, 'The Fundamental Rights case,' which he fought at the height of the Emergency. It was probably the longest case in the history of the Supreme Court and was heard by a Bench of judges for five months without interruption and they sat for five days a week. Nani won.

With all his achievements, the most endearing quality about Nani is his humility. When I asked him how he could remain so humble, he replied in one sentence, 'I was always aware of my own limitations.'

It is not common for a top-notch lawyer to join an industrial house the way Nani did. He said that Tata's did allow him to practice as and when he wished. Regarding his four decades in Bombay House, he says: 'I have never regretted it.'

Simple in his life, entirely satisfied to come to office in open-collared shirt and pants, he has given several crores of rupees to charity and it is unlikely that he has even kept an account of it. His last cheque was of a staggering amount—Rs 2 crore. 'I want to give away money in my lifetime. What is the use of bequeathing it because you are unable to take it away.' With all the eminence he has attained, he is still faithful to his childhood friends.

It is the tragedy of India that men like Nani, who should have graced the Parliament and held high offices, were not allowed the opportunity to serve the country to the extent they could have. Nevertheless, one should be grateful that we do have men like him who by the quality of their lives and their learning have set before the nation standards others could aspire to.

In 1991, Nani who kept fit with yoga, had a blocking of his arteries. I was shaken to see him a month after his bypass operation at the Royal Brompton in London. The spring in his step had gone; he walked slowly down the corridor of Bombay House. With great discipline and due to his evening walks he recouped and was back to his old self. But in 1997 and 1998 he had two mild strokes which curtailed his activities a great deal.

India's finest orator can no longer deliver speeches as he once did, but his affection for his friends, his desire to pitch in for public causes and his concern for his country remain unaffected. Though renowned throughout India, he remains modest about his accomplishments, 'I don't think I have reached any real position. In any case, whatever I have achieved is not due to my efforts. It is the blessing of providence.'

N.R. Narayana Murthy

My wife and I want our children to appreciate the importance of simplicity, hard work and money. We do all our household work ourselves—cleaning, washing clothes, shopping.

There is something fascinating about the life and personality of N.R. Narayana Murthy. The man who twenty years ago requested his wife for Rs 10,000 to kick-start his dream company, is today a billionaire. Despite Rs 2,500 crore of estimated worth, he has no servants at home and washes dishes and cleans the toilet. A role model for successful entrepreneurs, he has an ethical approach to life and despite the prominence and prosperity that he has achieved, he says his most prized possession is his 'conscience.'

Born in Mysore in 20 August 1946 to a schoolteacher, he had four brothers and three sisters. All of them used to stand first in class. Murthy qualified for a B. Tech course in the IIT but his father told him that with his salary of Rs 250 a month—about Rs 5,000 of today—he could not afford to spend Rs 100 on one child. Crestfallen, Murthy entered the local engineering college and graduated first class with distinction. That enabled him to win a scholarship at the IIT, Kanpur. In the 1960s, the Kanpur IIT was abuzz with the enthusiasm generated by young American professors from

Illustration by Gautam Roy

eight US universities. Kanpur IIT was set up with American assistance and US universities like the MIT took an interest in it. They gifted IIT with an IBM 7044 computer. And Murthy got hooked to it.

On passing out, Murthy turned down job offers from Air-India, Telco and HMT; instead, he chose to be the chief systems programmer at the IIM, Ahmedabad, at Rs 800 a month. It was, he now says, the best decision of his life. He was in charge of installing a Hewlett-Packard minicomputer. His chief, Prof. Krishnayya, observed, 'He picked up very well. He never asked how do I go about it? He just went ahead, did it.'

From there he went on to work in a non-profit organization, Systems Research Institute, in Pune and thereafter to the French software firm, SESA, in Paris. He picked up French and joined the team handling air cargo at the Charles de Gaulle Airport. His desire for social justice led him to accept Marxist ideas and at that time he considered himself a communist.

'What made you a communist?' I asked.

'It was in Nehru's time that we all had such leftist leanings. You remember the US refused us a steel plant. Russia came in. The Nehruvian influence was very strong at that time. There was no TV. The newspapers were all Indian. There were very few magazines to reflect pluralistic views. I had met no foreigner. And none of us had any responsibility for the creation of wealth. It all looked so idealistic—socialism, communism. So rosy.

'When I went to France in the early 1970s, it was the only Western country with a vibrant communist party. I realized even then that they believed that wealth had first to be created to be distributed.' For Murthy, the final disillusionment came en route to India.

Having finished his three-year term, he bought a haversack, packed his belongings, and with $425 decided to make his way from Paris to India by rail and road.

This journey marked another turning point in his life. While in the train to Sofia he was conversing with a French girl, not suspecting that the Bulgarian intelligence was keeping track. When the train pulled in at the station, he was arrested. He was incarcerated in the railway station room which was a mere 10 ft x 10 ft. Three days later they released him as he came 'from a friendly country'—India.

Murthy now says, 'If they were like this to a friend, what would they be to a foe?' This is when the last residue of empathy he had for Communism drained away. 'I realized the importance and freedom of speech, of opinion, and the freedom to do things according to your conscience. I also became more convinced about the need to minimize the role of government and ideology in the lives of people.' He adds, 'That also increased my faith in God.'

He arrived a year later in 1975, convinced that 'you cannot solve poverty by "isms" but by first creating wealth through legal and ethical means and then distributing it'.

While at the Systems Research Institute, he headed the software group of Putin Computer Systems, Pune, and in 1981 he and six of his software colleagues decided to establish Infosys Technologies Ltd. They were long on their plans, but short on funds. Their office was in Murthy's bedroom. With modest help from their wives, they launched their dream company. Conditions of control and shortages brought them soon down to earth.

While on a plane journey, he was fortunate enough to encounter the head of the Karnataka State Industrial

Development Corporation who invited him to establish his company in Bangalore. They acquired with the help of a finance institution their first computer worth Rs 52 lakh. They had an order of Rs 5 crore from the US for data processing but they couldn't get a telephone connection without a bribe. Murthy put his convictions into practice. He refused to bribe people. Instead, three of his colleagues worked on the project abroad.

'What,' I asked him, 'was the basis of your ethical approach? Which person influenced you?'

He replied promptly, 'Mahatma Gandhi and of course J.R.D. Tata. In my own opinion, he was the one person who ran his business ethically. There is hardly a week when my wife does not speak about him. The biggest conference hall at Infosys is named after J.R.D.'

'Has any book influenced you?' I asked him. He replied, '*Keynote—Speeches and Writings of J.R.D. Tata*. There are so many great ideas and great concepts in it. At one time there was hardly a week when I did not pick it up. Now, it is once in a quarter.'

He had a long way to go. Merely getting a licence to import a computer required frequent visits to Delhi. By 1989, one of the chosen six left for the US. In 1990 his colleagues and he took stock. There was gloom over the meeting. Murthy's colleagues contemplated selling out. As a mark of his faith in Infosys, Murthy offered to buy their shares and assured them that he saw better prospects ahead. His projection turned out to be true; the next year saw the liberalization budget of Manmohan Singh.

Restrictions on computer imports were lifted and foreign exchange curbs on companies were relaxed. The shackles that had bound them were broken. The Department of

Electronics under N. Vittal (later Central Vigilance Commissioner) emerged as a friend and not as a controller.

With liberalization came fresh challenges from the IBM and the US hardware and software giants. Murthy—as president of National Association of Software and Service Companies (NASSCOM)—refused to lobby the government to curb 100 per cent ownership by multinationals. The multinationals offered tantalizing salaries and Murthy and his friends decided they would prevent their talented staff from abandoning them by providing unrivalled work environment and benefits. In 1994, Murthy offered stock options to his people at a premium of Rs 85 a share. In the year 2000, the price of each share went as high as Rs 9,000. It is not just the money. It is the care he gives to his 'human assets', as he calls them. He gives them flexible hours of work, a recognition of their contribution, and the finest facilities of sport and games. 'My people get tired. I want them to be back fresh next morning,' he says. His vision is of a harmonious and happy team and he works for it. Infosys now has 8,910 employees and seventeen software development centres within India, spread across eight cities. With three development centres outside India—Toronto, Chicago and Croydon, UK—97 to 98 per cent of Infosys' spiralling income comes from exports.

International recognition came to Murthy when Nasdaq, the premier exchange for technology stocks, listed Infosys as its first Indian company in the American stock exchange. The American Depository Share (ADS) opened at $34 and grew ten times in value in a year's time. It gave other Indian companies a good start in US share markets.

His advice to people is, 'Early to bed and early to rise and work like hell.'

I said, 'I need your help. I have a problem. I go early to bed, but I can't get to rise early!'

He laughed heartily. 'Yours is an intellectual and creative activity which requires a different set of rules. We too like to think that what we do is creative but most of what we do is not. It is not like *Beyond the Last Blue Mountain* or *The Joy of Achievement*. When you get an idea, you have to get up and put it down.'

I inquired, 'You once pledged your wife's jewellery?'

He replied, 'In 1982, there was a delay in the receipt of a foreign payment and we had no money for salaries. We got the money in another six weeks. We have to meet our corporate obligations fully. If not, credibility goes down.'

What kind of a person is he? In spite of his abilities and renown he is an endearing and humble person. I had been of some help to him as I had given him significant quotations from J.R.D. Tata for his annual report of 1994/95. We arranged to meet at the guest house in Bangalore where we were staying. We were just shifting to the Bangalore Club. He kindly ferried us in his Esteem, driving the car himself. He came to our room, made sure we were well settled, asked if we liked the room, and went his way. The Bible speaks repeatedly of the shepherd who cares for his sheep. If he cared so much for us at our very first meeting, one can imagine what he is like with his own staff.

Murthy met his wife, Sudha Kulkarni, in Pune. Educated at the Indian Institute of Science, Bangalore, she was working at Telco. She could have made an excellent career woman but chose to stand by her husband and raise a daughter and a son. Now she looks after his foundation. They stay with their son (their daughter is studying in the US) at their old Jayanagar three-bedroom flat which he acquired with a loan of Rs 1 lakh. 'Both my wife and I believe we have to lead a natural life, which we have got used to as middle-class people. We want our children to appreciate the importance of simplicity, hard work and (the value of) money. We do all our household work ourselves—cleaning, washing clothes, shopping.'

'My regrets are: one, I have not spent enough time with my family; two, I did not do my Ph.D. though I had a fellowship; three, I did not become a teacher like my father, brother and brother-in-law; and four, I was not very aggressive during the first twelve years of this company.' And what does he wish to do when and if he retires? 'To become a teacher.'

He has only two weaknesses—books and Western music. His father too loved Western music. Murthy enjoys listening to Mozart, Bach, Beethoven and Johann Strauss.

What does he rank as his greatest achievement? 'Sustaining a value system in the company over the last twenty years.' He sums it up with the phrase, 'The softest pillow is a clear conscience.'

And how would he like to be remembered? 'As a fair person who prefers public good over private good.'

Sam Manekshaw

I take orders from only two ladies . . . my wife and the Prime Minister (Indira Gandhi).

The Japanese were advancing in Burma in early 1942. Defending the Sittand bridge was a twenty-eight-year-old captain. Following a hail of machine-gun bullets, the captain fell to the ground and was left for dead by the retreating forces. His orderly, who had effectively hidden himself during the engagement, came out after the Japanese left. He picked up his unconscious master and carried him on his shoulder the whole day, heading for the town of Prome. He hid the captain in ditches during air raids. When Captain Sam Manekshaw regained consciousness, he told his orderly, 'Leave me now and go, for I am finished. You should think of your wife and children and save your own life.'

'So long as there is life in you, I shall not leave you, Sir,' said Mehar Singh. For most of the next night he carried Manekshaw, bringing him to a field hospital. In a tent by candle light at 4 a.m., an Australian surgeon operated on Manekshaw and removed six bullets from his stomach, lungs and liver. Manekshaw was wrapped up in a blanket and sent off to Rangoon, towards which the Japanese were advancing.

At Rangoon, Manekshaw was told his case was hopeless. There was a ship leaving for Madras. 'If you ask to be put on

Illustration by Manjula Padmanabhan

the ship at your own risk, they might take you,' the officer advised. Manekshaw told the authorities, 'I am going to die in any case. I would rather die in India.' It was a dangerous journey across the Bay of Bengal but the ship was one of the last to arrive safely in Madras harbour. Manekshaw was taken to the general hospital where an operation saved his life. He was awarded the Military Cross, and spent the rest of the war as staff officer at Quetta. It is a wonder that Manekshaw lived. Destiny had a role reserved for him.

Born in 1914, Sam Manekshaw is the fifth in a family of four brothers and two sisters. Right from the time that he was a child, he had a fascination for the army and his ambition was to join it one day. His father was a medical practitioner at Amritsar. Manekshaw was educated at Nainital's Sherwood College from 1925 to 1930. After passing Senior Cambridge, he joined the Hindu Sabha College in Amritsar where he finished his Intermediate.

In 1932, Manekshaw appeared for King's Commission with the hope of going to Sandhurst. He was accepted, but, to his disappointment, from that year on Indians were not sent to Sandhurst but to the new Indian Military Academy at Dehra Dun. When he was commissioned in 1934, like all Indian officers of that period, he had to join a British regiment for six months. At the end of it, he joined the Fourth Battalion of the 12th Regiment of the Frontier Force. He spent his early career in the rugged North-West Frontier Province. Later, Manekshaw was GSO-1 in the Directorate of Military Operations in Delhi. The GSO-2 was an officer called Yahya Khan, who later became the President of Pakistan.

'Fear,' maintains Manekshaw, 'is a national phenomenon. A man who says he is not fearful is either lying or is a gurkha!

I am not a brave man. Please believe me. I get scared of ghosts and spirits. To fear is human, but if you are a leader, you must not show it.' He adds, 'During the World War II, I was commanding a Sikh company in Burma and I had a 6.2 feet jawan by the name of Sooraj Singh. He was a real badmaash. When his name came up for promotion, I turned it down. Later, a JCO came and told me, *Sahib gadbad ho gaya, Sooraj bolta hai ki aapko goli maarega.*' (Sahib, there is trouble, Sooraj says he'll shoot you.)

'I said, *Pesh karo.* (Present him.) And he was produced before me. I handed him a loaded pistol and told him to shoot me if he had the guts. He said *Sahib galti ho gaya.* (Sir, I've made a mistake.) I told him, *Dil nahin hai to bolo mat.*' (If you do not have the guts, don't talk.)

After World War II, Manekshaw held various assignments, one of the first being a tour of Australia to lecture on the Indian Army. In the years following Independence, he was posted at the war front in Jammu and Kashmir and for sometime was military adviser to the Indian delegation at the United Nations, when Kashmir was on its agenda.

He was sent to the British Imperial Defence College in 1957 and returned to become commandant of the Military Staff College at Wellington. When Indian defences cracked up under China's attack on NEFA (now Arunachal Pradesh), he was selected to become corps commander in that area. The confidence of the army was at its lowest. He distinguished himself by raising the morale of the troops and boosted their confidence in themselves and in their leadership.

Manekshaw had a way with his men; they trusted him. He was easily accessible not only to his troops but to everyone. Manekshaw notes, 'I am the people's general.'

From NEFA he was posted as GOC Western Command, and thereafter as GOC Eastern Command. On 8 June 1969 he became Chief of Staff of the Indian Army.

Manekshaw is a man with a happy temperament. He loves life. He has a strong streak of loyalty—loyalty to his superiors, his family, his nation. An Indian defence minister once asked Manekshaw for information on one of his senior officers. Politely but firmly he refused to give it. He aroused the wrath of the minister concerned and at one time it appeared that his career was finished. When the Chinese struck in 1962, the same defence minister left in disgrace and it was Manekshaw who was called upon to save the situation in NEFA.

He is disciplined in his personal life and keeps remarkably fit. Every morning his bearer knocks on his door at 5 o'clock with a cup of tea, whatever may be the time he retires to bed.

Manekshaw has a close-knit family and is 'wildly devoted' to his brothers and sisters who are proud of him. 'He is a kind man and we love him because of that,' said his brother Jan, 'and he has always got time for us.'

When the first Pakistani troops were captured in East Bengal, he immediately sent a message to his troops to treat them with dignity and humaneness, in accordance with the Geneva Convention.

I first met General Manekshaw when he was GOC, Eastern Command. Fort St. William in Calcutta, once the hub of the British Empire in India, was the headquarters of the General. The modest but well-painted building was superbly kept, all the brass was polished, and there was not a speck of dust or litter anywhere. The walls were tastefully decorated with sketches of Indian soldiers, from days gone by to the present times. Right from the orderly to the ADC everybody bustled about with zeal although it was peacetime. He inspired that kind of devotion.

Manekshaw was a rare combination of a first-class field commander and a good strategist. His modest height, daring and zest, reminds one of General Montgomery. But unlike Montgomery, he is a good listener. As Chief of the Army and later as Field-Marshal, he gave the impression of a man in command of himself and well in command of the men of whom he was justly proud. And his men, in turn, were proud of him.

Manekshaw had the highest respect for the fighting prowess of the Pakistan Army and refused to accept the theory that they did not fight the Bangladesh war vigorously enough. During one of his visits to a Pakistani prisoners-of-war camp, his officers wanted to accompany him for reasons of security. 'I am in my own country, I don't need protection,' he asserted. He went in with only his ADC to accompany him. He asked the Pakistanis whether they were comfortable or whether they had any complaints. He inspected their bunks, washrooms and kitchen. He spoke fluent Urdu which made the Pakistanis feel at home. He treated them as if they had not lost the war and as if they were his own troops. As he shook hands with the Pakistani subedar-major, the latter said in Urdu, 'We now see why you have such an excellent fighting force. I have been twenty-five years in the Pakistan army but no General has ever shaken my hand.'

A year after the famous Bangladesh victory, Manekshaw, told members of a Rotary conference in Kottayam at Kerala, 'There is much joy on this day but there is also much sorrow. In 1943, a beaten and a shaken Captain Manekshaw first spoke to the Rotary. Today, I command an excellent army. I have many nightmares. My army fought a gallant and tenacious armed force. Although the war lasted only fourteen days, 3,000 of my men were killed and over 8,500 wounded. I am glad 50 per cent of the wounded have been cured and have rejoined. But the remainder are maimed for life. Some will never walk, some will never see, some will be bedridden for life.'

He appealed for help for war widows and asked for employment opportunities for retrenched soldiers and officers. He is credited with putting the case of the servicemen so forcefully before a Pay Commission that it granted them a fair raise. A true soldier's war is never over.

Manekshaw has had a very poor opinion of most ministers he had worked with but had the highest respect for Indira Gandhi.

Manekshaw once recounted how in October 1970 Indira Gandhi undertook a diplomatic tour to present India's case to Western nations. About 10 million Bangladeshis had taken refuge in India. At a Cabinet meeting held when Indira Gandhi was abroad, General Manekshaw was summoned as the Chief of Staff of the Indian Army. One minister proposed that India should go to war on Indira's birthday, which was 19 November. Manekshaw said that was suicidal. 'It is the Id festival,' he explained. Manekshaw was grateful that India had an astute prime minister like Mrs Gandhi. Incidentally, Mrs Gandhi and Manekshaw enjoyed a good personal equation. They respected and trusted each other and in a war such an equation is of the utmost importance. When I met him at a party after the war, he regaled a group of women with the words, 'I take orders from only two ladies—my wife and the prime minister.'

Manekshaw has two daughters. After retirement, he

became an avid gardener at his home in Conoor. His wife said he was at first impatient at the slow growth of the flowers and plants in the garden. He, who once ordered a million men could not coax a modest plant to grow faster. From Conoor, he frequently motors down Coimbatore to fly to attend board meetings in various cities for he is a director of many companies. Though he is in his mid-eighties, his zest for life is undiminished.

Sucheta Kripalani

Gandhiji said if you remain unhappy it will oppress Kripalani; so you must marry someone else.

'I was dark, dull, agonizingly shy,' Sucheta Kripalani wrote about herself as a child. How she changed into a bold individual who defied the Mahatma for her loved one, and later rose to be chief minister, is an absorbing story.

Sucheta Roy was educated in Loreto Convent at Simla. It was there that a teacher called Mrs Roy praised and encouraged her, as a result of which Sucheta overcame her shyness and got to enjoy her studies. From then on, she decided to work hard and her performance steadily improved.

Born in 1908, she came from a large Bengali family belonging to the Brahmo Samaj sect. Her father, a doctor, being in government service, could not take an active part in the freedom struggle but he and his children were heart and soul for it.

When Sucheta shifted to Queen Mary School in Delhi, an incident took place of which she was ashamed for a long time. The girls in her school were asked to turn up in honour of the Prince of Wales. The Congress had called for a boycott of the Prince's visit. Sucheta and her sister, Sulekha, were upset at the idea of going out to honour the Prince of Wales

Illustration by Manjula Padmanabhan

and stand in the garden at Alipore Road. But they did not pick up sufficient courage to refuse to do so. 'After reaching the gardens, in the confusion, we two made ourselves scarce and sat behind the bush till the whole thing was over, and then joined the girls to walk back to school. But this did not absolve our conscience of our feeling of shame. We both felt very small because of our own cowardice.' Sucheta's boldness later may have had something to do with her anger at her own conduct at that early age.

Sucheta was studying for her MA in history when, shortly before her examination, her father died. In spite of the shock, Sucheta appeared for the finals and stood first in history. She was awarded the Gold Medal. To help look after her family, she started working at a school in Lahore. Later, she joined the teaching staff at Benares Hindu University.

A few years later, in 1934, Bihar was struck by an earthquake and it was there that she first came across stark poverty which shook her. 'One day we came to a small hut the size of a large kennel; the door was a small hole through which one could just crawl in and out. We could hear some sounds, but no one would come out. So I peeped into the opening and saw an old woman sitting completely naked. She could not come out even to beg as she had no clothes! We gave her the nicest sari we had. Her existence had already reached rock-bottom. She has lost nothing on account of the earthquake!'

Earlier at Benares, she had got to know Acharya Kripalani, twenty years her senior. As she became involved in the Independence struggle, she saw more of Kripalani and they grew fond of each other. Gandhiji could not hear the thought of 'losing his national worker' (J.B. Kripalani) to the charms of domestic life. He stoutly opposed the marriage, but chose to deal with Sucheta rather than with Kripalani. After much persuasion, Sucheta decided to forgo the marriage.

Next day, the Mahatma called her again. He said, 'If you remain unhappy, it will oppress Kripalani; so you must marry someone else.' At this outrageous suggestion Sucheta turned on him and told him in no uncertain terms that what he proposed was 'wrong, unjust and immoral'.

To make things more difficult for Sucheta, Kripalani's sister reacted adversely to the idea of her sadhu brother (he was far from one!) marrying in his late forties. Sucheta's mother too opposed the marriage because she wanted a life of security and comfort for her daughter and Kripalani was unlikely to offer either.

Fortunately for the couple, Jamnalal Bajaj (whom Gandhiji called his fifth son), intervened on Sucheta's behalf. Then Gandhiji called Sucheta and told her he had no objection to the marriage but he could not give his blessings. He could 'only pray' for them. The Acharya recalls how Sucheta won the heart of her husband's family who had opposed the marriage. In years to come Sucheta would always bring his family gifts.

The Acharya told me he could not fathom what Sucheta saw in him—a 'distinguished vagabond', as poetess Sarojini Naidu once called him.

Kripalani was then the Congress general secretary and stayed at Swaraj Bhavan. 'Sucheta brought some pots and pans from her Benares home to add to the meagre stock I had of them... She did not know much cooking. She learnt some of it from me,' Kripalani once said.

Sucheta once wrote how influenced she was by her husband in the early years of marriage. She first adopted his style of speaking and thinking, but later she branched out on her own. And the credit for it goes as much to her husband as to her, for he did not seek to dominate or overawe her.

'Sucheta could have helped me in my work as general secretary to the Congress. But I did not want her to do that. It would not have led to the full utilization of her talents, which at that time only I knew. I wanted her to follow her own bent in life and to grow,' Kripalani said.

She was put in independent charge of the foreign department of the Congress. In the Quit India days, Sucheta was not immediately arrested and had an exciting time helping with an underground transmitting station in Bombay. She had some hairbreadth escapes. Travelling on a train one day, she realized she was being watched by secret servicemen who were waiting to execute the warrant of arrest pending against her. She took a woman passenger into confidence, discarded her khadi clothes, donned a sari, and gave the policemen the slip.

Sucheta's courage was staggering. In 1943, when she heard of the Mahatma's marathon fast while he was in jail at Aga Khan's Palace in Poona, she was so stirred that she walked into the office of the home secretary of the Bombay government and asked for permission to see the Mahatma. The Home Secretary, H.V.R. Iyengar, was so impressed with her guts that he asked the Governor to grant her request. The British police commissioner of Bombay was eager to arrest her. But his hands were stayed. She was not only given safe conduct but the Governor also ensured she was not followed for twenty-four hours after the interview. The British 'played the game'.

As the day of Independence approached, communal frenzy engulfed Bihar and Bengal. In the Noakhali area of East Bengal, women were being kidnapped and raped.

Undaunted by the volatile situation, Kripalani and Sucheta went to prepare the way for Gandhiji's historic visit. Kripalani soon left to report to Gandhiji, leaving his wife behind. Sucheta did not tell her husband then that she had procured some arsenic and kept it handy in case she was attacked.

For eight months Sucheta stood her ground, till the situation was brought under control. Sucheta was then barely forty years old but the villagers out of respect for her called her mataji, mother.

On their return to Delhi, the Kripalanis found that refugees were streaming in from the other side of India—Punjab. Sucheta threw herself into relief work. She appealed on the radio for cooked food from Delhi citizens and the food came. She had some old barracks painted at her own cost to house refugees.

She and her husband were both elected to the Constituent Assembly and in the first parliamentary elections, as a result of her work with the refugees, she was elected to Parliament.

Just prior to the 1952 elections, the Acharya and Sucheta were disillusioned with the Congress and formed their own party. The Acharya was never to return to the Congress fold, but five years later, Sucheta again displayed her independent spirit. She felt it would be more constructive if she rejoined the ruling party.

Eight years later, in spite of Nehru's reservations, the Congress Parliamentary Board supported Sucheta's candidature for chief ministership of Uttar Pradesh—the most populous state of India. She was efficient and compassionate, sometimes to the point of weakness. A senior civil servant, K.K. Dass, who served her, gave a frank evaluation of her performance as chief minister from 1963 to

1967 in his book, *Sucheta—An Unfinished Autobiography*.

Between 1901 and 1963, the irrigated area of Uttar Pradesh remained constant. In her three and a half years of chief ministership, it was increased by 25 per cent through minor irrigation projects. On the debit side, her leniency towards government servants on strike was to prove costly not only to her state but also to other states.

'Setting her weaknesses alongside her strong points, the mixture resulted in the best chief minister Uttar Pradesh has had: clear-sighted, honest and as firm as her humaneness would allow,' said Dass.

Till the Congress split in 1969, Sucheta remained in the Congress while her husband was a leader of the Opposition. The Acharya was squarely criticized for this, 'Even his wife does not agree with him.' Sucheta faced a similar charge, 'Even her husband does not agree with her.' In the last five years of her life, they were once again politically united.

In April 1978, when I asked the Acharya whether their political differences ever affected their domestic life, he replied, 'No. In a democracy, there are no such great differences of ideology or conviction.' Perhaps it is more true to say that their affection for each other was greater than their political differences could ever be.

Sucheta was a kind-hearted woman, humble and attentive. Power never intoxicated her. Her husband related how till the end people came to her for help 'with all sorts of cock-and-bull stories of distress. Somebody said he was robbed in the train of his cash, his ticket and his luggage. He was given his railway fare . . . She would not deny help to anyone in need.'

When some of the supplicants would return to her for more favours, Sucheta would get angry. At this point, the

Acharya would smile and say, 'Where else will they go?' He was opposed to this kind of giving.

The Acharya's orderly mind believed in organized charities and he and his wife set up charitable trusts to the tune of Rs 1,50,000, say Rs 1 crore in today's terms. But Sucheta also gave a lot to individuals who came to her with tales of distress. In the late evening of his life, when Sucheta was no more, the Acharya admitted to me, 'I think she was right and I was wrong. It kept her heart soft and tender and responsive to human misery and suffering.' Could it be that the sight of the destitute woman in a hut in Bihar made such an indelible impact on her that she could never turn away from the needy?

Sucheta never harboured a grudge for injuries done to her. Then, she was a patron of the fine arts. Her only relaxation was an occasional film or an evening recital. She sang beautifully, specially Tagore's songs. On 15 August 1947, as independence was ushered in, at the momentous session of Parliament, she was one of the two to be selected to sing *Vande Mataram*.

Sucheta was ever ready to serve. Even as chief minister she would insist on arranging the room for her guest. After a heavy day's work, she would wake up twice at night to ensure that her husband—if ailing—was comfortable.

Those who had the privilege of being invited by the Kripalanis to their home in Sarvodaya Enclave, New Delhi, will long remember the fiery old man and the quiet, gracious woman who served the tea.

Vijay Merchant

My philosophy is learnt from cricket: the better batsman takes care of the weaker one if your side is to win.

When I got to know Vijay Merchant in the 1970s, his batting average in first-class cricket stood next only to that of Don Bradman. Bradman's average was 95.14 runs and Vijay's was 72.74. He was about seventy years of age and I expected to find him a man nostalgic about his past. Instead, I found him looking forward to the future. 'I am interested in what happens next. The past is only important in so far as I can learn from my mistakes,' he said.

He had found a new purpose, but before we come to that, let us first dwell on cricket.

Many fondly remember that stylish batsman who played with such ease and precision at Brabourne Stadium, Bombay. Vijay Merchant is perhaps the greatest name in Indian cricket between the age of C.K. Naidu and the era of Gavaskar. The tall and impressive C.K. 'concentrated on the game as nobody does, and he inspired me', says Vijay. C.K. was obsessed with physical fitness 'and it was as an athlete that we first heard of him'. The discipline of C.K. created a profound impact on young Vijay, whose career was opening as C.K.'s was closing.

'Who among the foreign cricketers impressed you? What

Illustration by Manjula Padmanabhan

about Bradman?' I asked.

'Our paths never crossed. But I did play against Hammond twice, in 1936 and 1946,' he replied.

'What impressed you about Hammond?' I inquired.

'He was a classic batsman; he was consistent,' Vijay said.

Vijay's two spells against England established him in world-class cricket. In 1946, as vice-captain during a wet summer, he knocked 2,385 runs (74.53 average) with two double centuries—242 not out against Lancashire and 205 against Sussex. But Vijay's first steps on the ladder to fame were taken at the school nets in Bombay.

Vijay was educated at Bharda New High School, Bombay, and he started playing cricket at the age of nine. He remembers gratefully the interest taken by his joint principal, Kaikobad Marzban, who came to the nets daily with the boys. But there was no formal coaching as at present. Vijay observed minutely and picked up the game. 'I avoided bad habits at the nets—I never gave away my wicket, did not try fancy strokes, concentrated on the ball one hundred per cent, did not lift the ball in the air and generally batted most seriously,' he said.

To these guidelines he added one more—to train at the nets and practise. This is what he says, 'Playing against bumpers and beamers at the nets made me realize that even more important than hitting those balls was developing the art of getting out of the line of the ball, so that, that particular ball would be absolutely innocuous. When I realized that, in order to bowl that kind of a ball the bowler had to exert three times the energy he would spend in bowling a normal ball, it made me concentrate more on the art of leaving such a ball than playing it. Thus, both the ability to leave the ball and the ability to hit a bumper came to me most emphatically at the practice nets itself and, since my matchplay was an extension of what I did at the nets, it made me feel absolutely comfortable against that particular kind of bowling.'

After finishing school, Vijay took commerce at Sydenham College and later joined his family concern of Thackerseys, a textile company that ran Hindoostan Mills. He played the Ranji Trophy where he hit his highest score of 359 runs at Brabourne Stadium. In those days the popular Test matches were played between four teams and were called Quadrangular, later Pentangular. The Quadrangular were among the Hindu XI, the Muslim XI, the Parsi XI, the European XI. Later, the Rest XI were added, and it became a Pentangular.

Brabourne Stadium's first stand, on the west side, was for the Islam Gymkhana, next was the Parsi Gymkhana, then was a larger stand, the Hindu Gymkhana, and thereafter were the massive northern and eastern stands. In most finals, the Hindu XI played the Muslim XI. Excitement was considerable in the stands of the Muslim and Hindu Gymkhana but the Parsis in-between kept the rivalry in check! Later, after Partition, matches which aroused communal feelings were discontinued.

Vijay played in the Quadrangular, the Pentangular, and in the Test matches. One-day matches had not been thought of then. To Vijay, the game of cricket was the pursuit of excellence. 'An innings by Merchant grows: it sprouts. No exotic bloom but its construction is perfect to the last detail,' wrote John Arlott.

Rusi Modi, who opened the innings for India against England in 1946, says that the nearest approach to Vijay's style was Sir Len Hutton's, 'Vijay had no apparent weakness. In an innings by Merchant every fine point of batsmanship was on view to evoke admiration. The latest of late cuts and the finest leg glance came naturally to him. Merchant was a rhythmically disciplined batsman. I was indeed lucky in having Vijay as my partner on several occasions. He made the bowling look easy. This inspired great confidence in me. Vijay went out of his way to help his contemporaries and each one of us played better in his company.'

That was true sportsmanship. Vijay made others great. In his lifetime, Vijay was the only Indian to score 2,000 runs in an English season. His average in first-class cricket of 72.74 runs in 221 innings was excelled by his own average of 98 runs in 47 innings of the Ranji Trophy. His first-class cricket career was made up of 12,876 runs and 43 centuries.

Most batsmen of his day tried to model their play on Vijay's classic and correct style, but few attained his stature. It is said, 'The style is the man.' Vijay had taken the trouble to streamline his entire life to one goal.

'I had to remain at all times perfectly fit—light on my feet, quick in my reflexes, supple on my toes . . . For this purpose, I had to run long distances, skip a thousand times a day, play gruelling games of squash and build my stamina for extensive innings at the crease,' Vijay said.

For mental alertness, Vijay refrained from smoking and drinking. To maintain his weight, he avoided greasy and starchy food.

A batsman has to judge a ball travelling at a speed of over eighty miles per hour. It pitches fifteen feet from the batsman, who has just that split-second to decide whether to play it aggressively or defensively, or let it pass, or get out of its way.

Reflexes depend on the eye and then on the brain. To keep his eyes peeled, Vijay never wore coloured glasses when off the crease. He saw as few films as possible and always read under adequate lighting. For his general fitness he followed the adage 'early to bed and early to rise . . .' Cricketer Rusi Modi recalled that in 1946, on the eve of the final Test between England and India, at Kennington Oval, he went to Vijay's room for a chat. After talking to him for a couple of minutes, Vijay said, 'I want an early night as I must score a century tomorrow.' Modi ventured to suggest that his chances of scoring a hundred were not too bright as he would have to encounter bowlers on a rain-affected wicket. With a smile over that deep cut in his chin, Vijay retorted, 'So what?' As things turned out, Vijay scored a magnificent 128 in this Test.

He retired from first-class cricket at the age of forty-one. Till he was sixty-four, his long sight was a perfect 6/6. 'Just as bad habits do not leave you, good habits also do not forsake you,' he said. Good habits, he believed, trained your reflexes and even when concentration occasionally failed, say in car-driving, your reflexes automatically did the right thing.

Was he ever nervous before going to the crease?

The answer is 'Yes'. Many years ago, he confided to the great cricketer, Duleepsinghji, that he felt tense before a match right up to the point he went to the crease and the umpire gave him the guard. Only when the bowler started his run did nervousness leave Vijay. Duleepsinghji assured him it was not 'nervousness' but 'nervous tension' that gripped Vijay, and added that every great sportsman must have that nervous tension to build up the concentration so necessary to succeed. Those who feel confident are the people who fail to concentrate hundred per cent and miss out.

In *The Complete Who's Who of Test Cricketers*, C.

Martin-Jenkins writes glowingly about Vijay Merchant,

> His cutting, both square and leg, was brilliant, and he hooked, drove (especially the fast bowlers) and played the ball off his legs with masterful certainty . . . There was something feline about him at the wicket . . .

Vijay's cricketing career started from 1929, when he was only eighteen, and lasted till 1951. When that period ended, he moved happily to the next phase of his life, just doing good to people.

'Life,' he says, 'is my great teacher. I have never read a book except on cricket. My social welfare work is learnt from people.' A man from Satara district told me of the help Vijay had given him. One day a village girl collapsed at his doorstep in Satara. He took the girl to a local doctor who diagnosed very advanced TB. The Good Samaritan hardly knew Vijay but nonetheless appealed to him for help. Vijay responded immediately and cabled to inform him that he had secured the girl's admission to a TB hospital. Vijay monitored her progress for months. Even when she was well on the way to recovery, he still corresponded about her rehabilitation. Though he was not a formal social worker, ordinary people came to him with their dreams and sorrows, walked into his heart and there they abided, while he wrestled for a solution to their problems—be it a physical disability or a family problem.

Having considerable resources, Vijay felt he was blessed and owed something to the less fortunate. At his family's Hindoostan Mills, he established a welfare centre well-staffed with a health officer and a social worker. To their credit, his family members supported him. Twice a week, he was available to anyone between eleven and one in the mornings. If a blind person came and Vijay found him or her competent enough to sell cloth from door to door, he encouraged the person to go into business, initially with cloth worth Rs 100, from the sale of which the person could earn Rs 19.

If they did not have the initial amount, the mill would advance the cloth. Seven out of ten people did not return for the next instalment of cloth. But Vijay was undeterred, 'If three out of ten get rehabilitated, I am satisfied.'

Vijay gave unstinted care, the kind which even the British National Health Service would hesitate to extend. Once a blind or a deaf person came under his care, he would even consider their matrimonial needs. Occasionally, he found the couple a room to stay! Once moved by a blind couple, when the wife cooked a meal for him, Vijay managed to procure for them a Burshane stove, which in those days was difficult to get, and a cylinder. He took care to remember the names of their children. They were his extended family.

'Have you been able to enthuse others in your circle of friends to do the same work that you do?' I asked him.

'They give donations but do not share the same objectives,' he replied.

It is not a small thing to take people into your heart. Once Mrs Nasrullah, the then sheriff of Bombay, asked Vijay to give shelter to a girl of eighteen as her father had behaved brutally towards her. He first said, 'No, I'll give money but not shelter.' But when he heard the girl's story, he arranged for an elderly woman to take charge of her. The young girl began to help at his Health Centre, giving milk to those workers in the factory who suffered from TB. Then, she, a Hindu, fell in love with a Muslim. One day she came to Vijay and confided in him. As it was a delicate matter, Vijay involved Mrs Nasrullah again. The sheriff advised the couple to wait for six months and, if their affection for each other still endured, to get married. At the end of six months, the couple said they still loved each other.

To be accepted by the boy's family and community, the girl had to become a Muslim. When Vijay wanted to arrange her marriage at his factory, he was advised by some not to do so. 'If I cannot do so, then my whole philosophy of life has failed,' he said. He went ahead with his plans. A Qazi came and performed the marriage and asked Vijay to sign as the girl's father. At first, Vijay, a Hindu, flatly refused. But then he realized that for all practical purposes, the girl had no father and so he signed the marriage register. 'They have two lovely children now,' Vijay told me proudly.

'Why do you do this kind of social work?' I inquired.

'My philosophy,' replied Vijay, 'is learnt from cricket: the better batsman takes care of the weaker one if your side is to win.' For example, he added, 'I would like my son to marry a poor girl, not a rich girl.'

'Secondly, God has been so good to me. How do I repay his debt? I am not religious, I never go to a temple. But my faith in God is strong.'

'Has it always been so?' I asked him.

'From the beginning, but naturally it develops. I feel what I do for people is my worship to God,' Vijay answered. After living a life rich in experience, Vijay died on 27 October 1987.

Vinoba Bhave

I know no other technique but love for I do not believe in force.

A man wearing only a loincloth and a green peak cap was squatting on the ground, pulling out weeds. He was told the next visitor had arrived. He rose to walk into his sparsely furnished room.

Crude pieces of wood nailed together made up his bed. Only a piece of cloth lay on it and a couple of thick volumes. There was no pillow but the bed was slightly inclined, so he could rest and read.

Vinoba Bhave was Gandhiji's favourite disciple. Known the world over as 'the walking saint', between 1951 and 1970 he collected 4.2 million acres of land from about a million donors, to be distributed to landless families. By 1970, Vinoba had helped to distribute more land than the combined state governments of India.

The saga of the land donation mission, Bhoodan, began in 1951 in Andhra Pradesh. Prem Vaidya, writing on *Vinoba: The Man and his Mission,** recalls,

There was widespread violence in Telengana. Vinoba

---
* *Imprint*, April 1982.

Illustration by Manjula Padmanabhan

decided to study the root of the problem. He visited the village of Pochampalli, 3,000 landless people: 40 Harijan families. He entered a Harijan hut and was overwhelmed by the poverty. He asked the Harijans what would alleviate their plight. They replied, 'Land'.
'How much land?' asked Vinoba.
'Eighty acres.'
'Let us try.'

That evening, Vinoba addressed the entire village in a simple, heartfelt manner, 'I visited some poor brothers of yours who have no food to eat nor any land to till. They are dying for no fault of theirs. Could some of you be willing to share your riches and save them?' Vinoba's eyes searched the crowd for a man who would come forth. His eyes fell upon a neatly dressed man, Ramachandra Reddy, a landlord. Ramachandra got up and asked: 'How much?' Vinoba answered, '100 acres'. Then and there Ramachandra wrote out the deed and signed it, and thus the Bhoodan movement was born.

For fourteen years he walked twelve to fifteen miles a day from village to village. He woke up at 4 a.m. and often by sunrise he was on the road. At his evening meetings, along with bhajans and prayers, he spoke to thousands. Some walked many miles to see this holy man. Others came with their families, in bullock-carts, to get a glimpse of him. To those gathered, he often said, 'I have come to rob you with love. I want you to change your heart and part with your surplus land so those who haven't any can get it.'

People signed papers saying that they would turn over their land. Sometimes whole villages gave up their property rights and decided on community ownership. Thousands of

Sarvodaya workers systematically followed up his programme.

I asked him, 'If you had to live your life all over again, would you do the same?' He answered, 'I know no other technique but love for I do not believe in force. The results are much better than the effort I put in. I have served God little but He has rewarded me bountifully. If I go again, I can only ask with love . . .'

After 1970 Vinoba withdrew from active life, although he retained his links with the Sarvodaya movement. He stayed at an ashram in Paunar at Wardha with about thirty other inmates, mostly women, who had decided to remain celibate. He spent his time walking, reading and cleaning up the place.

His meals were simple, comprising papaya, jaggery and milk curdled with lime. In-between, after about every half-hour, he drank water. He was quite fit except for occasional attacks of vertigo.

Vinoba answered no mail. If anyone wanted to see him, the place to go to was Paunar, via Nagpur.

There was a twinkle in his eyes when I met him at Paunar Ashram one morning in 1972. He lifted his dark glasses to read my questions. He was by then stone-deaf, so all questions were written down. He insisted that they be addressed to him in the Devanagiri script. He felt that English as well as all Indian languages should be written in the Devanagiri script as he felt that would 'unify India'. 'I am a faddist and I have found a new fad,' he went on to explain.

'Europe has a common market but it first had a common script (Roman). In India, we do not have a common script although 40 per cent of the words in the four languages of south India are the same as in the rest of India,' he said.

His assistant, Gautam Bajaj, a grandson of Jamnalal Bajaj, pulled out a Telugu book in the Telugu script and a Telugu book in the Devanagiri script. Vinoba got me to compare the two, and added, 'Baba (as he called himself) learnt English and French in school but soon picked up German and Latin and Esperanto because the script was the same.' He felt if a common script was evolved, it would be easier for an Indian to learn any language in his country.

Vinoba Bhave was born in a Brahmin family in Maharashtra in September 1895. From childhood, he showed a remarkable lack of interest in worldly affairs and gave up his college studies because the education he received did not fulfil the hunger of his spirit. So he went to Benares to study Sanskrit and philosophy and to lead a life of contemplation and brahmacharya.

He was torn between two urges. One was to work for the freedom of his country as a terrorist. The other drew him towards the Himalayas, the traditional home of spiritual seekers. While still undecided, Vinoba came in touch with Mahatma Gandhi, who in his own life synthesized the urge to fight for freedom with the desire to live on a spiritual plane.

Vinoba was among the first to join Mahatma Gandhi's Sabarmati Ashram at Ahmedabad. He was not too widely known in India till 1940. Gandhiji wrote an article entitled, 'Who is Vinoba Bhave?' to introduce him to the country.

Gandhiji envisaged not only a free India but also the creation of a new social order, different from the capitalist, socialist or communist systems. It was to be a society based on love and human values: decentralized, self-governing, non-exploitative. Its name, Sarvodaya, meant 'uplift of all', a society for the good of all. When Gandhiji died, Vinoba decided to fulfil that dream. Its practical evolution he sought in the Bhoodan movement. Jayaprakash Narayan called it 'the first attempt in history to bring about a social revolution and reconstruction by means of love'.

J.P. added, 'Vinoba is not a politician, nor a social reformer or revolutionary. He is first and last a man of God. He endeavours every second to blot himself out, to make himself so empty that God may fill him up and make him His instrument.'

To visit Vinoba in the ashram was a humbling experience. Apart from the distinctive personality of the man and his humanity which came through, it was an amazing experience to go through books that had been produced as a result of his speeches, lectures and study. The breadth of his knowledge was astounding for he had studied and published a series of books on the essence of the great religions. For his study of the Koran, he learnt Arabic. Perhaps his best known work is *Talks on the Gita*.

One of his close colleagues, Shriman Narayan, later the Governor of Gujarat, said, 'I do not have a shadow of doubt that even when the traces of his Bhoodan movement will be hard to detect by research scholars, his discussion on the *Gita* would shine out for centuries to come as the glittering jewels of a great rishi who lived in flesh and blood on Indian soil.'

Vinoba's commentary on the *Gita*, of which more than two and a half million copies have been sold in Indian and the European languages, was a fallout of the talks given to prisoners when he was in jail between February and June 1932. On eighteen successive Sundays, he delivered discourses in order to give faith and knowledge to the prisoners.

Twice a day Vinoba and his ashram inmates sat together and prayed and meditated for fifteen minutes. 'I like silence very much. God gives his *bhaktas* direction through the inner voice.' Absolute purity, he said, 'is God's', meaning, it comes from God.

Although he knew so many European languages, Vinoba had never been abroad. Going by his ways and appearance, one could mistake him for a man belonging to an ancient era. But in many ways he was more up to date than most.

J.P. once talked about a meeting between Vinoba Bhave and Mrs Martin Luther King, 'When Mrs King was introduced as a great singer and a friend suggested that she should sing for Vinoba, everyone was delighted. I looked at Vinoba and wondered if he knew what Negro spirituals were. We were all startled, most of all the Americans, when Vinoba, as if in answer, raised his ever-downcast eyes towards Mrs King and intoned softly, "Were you there, were you there when they crucified my Lord?" When Mrs King sang that song, it had an added poignancy for us.'

By the time I met him, Vinoba could not hear at all. On that particular day the renowned singer, M.S. Subbulakshmi, was also in the ashram during prayer time at 10.30 a.m. She sang *shlokas* of Vishnu Sahasranam. Lost in worship, as Subbulakshmi sang, Vinoba merrily tapped his hands on his knees and thigh, to keep time.

'How can he keep rhythm when he cannot hear?' I asked myself. A deaf Beethoven had to bang at his piano. To my amazement, Vinoba knew exactly when the *shlokas* came to an end, and folded his hands in homage to God.

In early November 1982 Vinoba stopped taking food and water as he wanted to go to his Creator. For eight days this process, called santhara among the Jains, continued. He even stopped talking. All he did was to recite God's name, 'Ram, Hari.' On 15 November 1982, he went to meet his Maker.

Zakir Husain

I shall do my utmost to take our people towards what Gandhiji strove restlessly to achieve—a pure life, individual and social, an insistence on the means being pure as the end, an active and sustained sympathy for the weak and downtrodden, and a fervent desire to forge unity among the diverse sections of the Indian people.

It was 25 April 1968.

Seven rugged-looking characters, ranging in age from seventeen to sixty, entered the gates of Rashtrapati Bhavan for an appointment with the President of India. Among them were former purse-snatchers, drunkards, and gamblers who had changed their ways and become responsible citizens. They were some of the Dalits who lived in a slum colony in New Delhi. 'I hear a lot of things are going on in your area,' the President said. 'I would like to know about them.' Sensitively, he drew out from them how they had stopped gambling, drinking and quarrelling with each other and how they were keeping their area clean. At the end, their spokesman said to the President, 'We are honoured to meet a great man like you.'

The President replied, 'I am very fortunate in meeting men like you this afternoon. One does not have this sort of experience often in a lifetime. Just as evil catches on, so does good, and I have caught a lot of it from you this afternoon.'

Dr Zakir Husain accorded these men the same courtesy he would have shown to a Head of State. He meant it when he said, 'The whole of India is my home. Its people are my family.'

Dr Zakir Husain was born in Hyderabad in 1897. His father, Fida Husain, a successful lawyer, died when Zakir was eight years old. His mother returned to her father's home in Uttar Pradesh and put Zakir in a school at Etawah. When Zakir was fourteen years old, his mother and most members of his family died of bubonic plague. Only two of his brothers survived.

Shortly after, he was placed in the care of a distant relative, a Sufi by the name of Hasan Shah. After completing his schooling, young Zakir went to Aligarh University. As a student, he was a good debater and also contributed to the college magazine. He would walk to the railway station to get the first copy of the daily paper and would read it aloud to his friends, adding his comments. He continued to be a voracious reader.

In 1920, Gandhiji called for non-cooperation, and asked students and professors to leave government-sponsored educational institutions. Zakir responded to this call. 'It was the first conscious decision of my life. Perhaps the only one I have ever taken. The rest of my life has but flowed from it.'

Gandhiji was keen to start national educational institutions, and some, like Kashi Vidyapeeth, were set up. Zakir and his friends set up Jamia Millia Islamia—the Muslim National University—first in Aligarh; later it was shifted to Delhi.

In 1922, Zakir went to Europe and studied economics at Berlin University. He worked hard and earned his Ph.D. He

Illustration by Manjula Padmanabhan

grew to love classical Western music and the German language, which he read almost daily for the rest of his life. He wrote a book in German on Gandhiji. He returned to India with a Ph.D. and from then on was known as Dr Zakir Husain. He observed humorously, 'When I sometimes go to my native village, I am asked to give medical advice. The designation of doctor attached to my name is impossible to explain away!'

From 1926 to 1948, Dr Husain struggled to put Jamia Millia Islamia on its feet. Its twin aims were to provide education along Islamic precepts, and to inculcate nationalism in its pupils.

Funds were scarce and as vice-chancellor, Dr Husain had to bear the responsibility of raising them. He had a passion for cleanliness and often picked up pieces of paper and rags, littering the premises, as an example to his pupils. Every week, he inspected the kitchens.

During this period Dr Zakir Husain become interested in Gandhiji's concept of basic education which meant teaching pupils through manual labour. He grew in stature as an educationist. He stuck to education when others were drifting into the vortex of politics. He defined an educated man as one who 'has no blinkers . . . is not conceited, is not a hardboiled egg, is not an internally dissipated busybody'.

Remaining aloof from politics did not mean that he remained distant from national life. In a stirring convocation address in 1935, he told the graduates, 'The country to which you will go from here is a very unfortunate country. It is a country of slaves, of illiterates; a country of injustice and oppression, of cruel customs and ignorant worshippers; a country of fraternal hatred and of disease, of laziness, of poverty, of despair, of hunger and of calamities. In short, it is a cursed country. But, after all, it is our country. We have to live in it and die in it. That is why this country will be a challenge to your abilities, and the test of your love.'

He warned students that they may be tempted to destroy the society which permits such a State. 'I believe that destruction will not ease our work. Destruction is there already in abundance. The country needs not the spurt of your blood, but the steady flow of your perspiration at all times.'

The years between 1940 and 1947 were difficult ones for nationalist Muslims like him. They had to face the verbal assault of the Muslim League which called them 'traitors' to their community.

When the Congress proposed to put Dr Husain's name forward for a Cabinet seat in the Interim Union Government of 1946, he said he would only agree if he was unanimously backed by the Muslim Leaguers as well—which he was not.

Dr Husain would have no part in anything approaching sordidness. He fought the communal hatred that was engulfing the subcontinent. Not long before Partition, at the silver jubilee celebrations of the Jamia Millia Islamia, he got on a common platform men like M.A. Jinnah, Jawaharlal Nehru, Liaquat Ali Khan, Maulana Azad and C. Rajagopalachari. He spoke with anguish: 'The fire of hatred is burning in a noble human land, for God's sake sit together and extinguish the fire of hatred. This is not the time to ask who is responsible for it and what is its cause. The fire is raging. Please extinguish it. The problem is not of this community's or that community's survival. It is the choice between civilized human life and barbarism. For God's sake, do not allow the very foundations of civilized life in this country to be destroyed.'

A year later, in the wake of Partition, he would have been killed at Ludhiana station had it not been for a Sikh and a Hindu who rescued him. 'It is intolerable to me,' said Gandhiji, 'that a man like Maulana Sahib (Abul Kalam Azad) or Dr Husain should not be able to move about in Delhi as freely and with as much safety as myself.' A few days later, Gandhiji was assassinated.

Aligarh, Dr Husain's old university, had come under a cloud of suspicion and he was urged to become its vice-chancellor. The years 1948-50 were difficult ones for him.

In 1949, he had his first heart attack. He was advised by his doctor to sit in the sunshine, and as he did so, he watched the gardeners tend the roses. His love for roses stayed with him till he died and he often tended them himself in the mornings at Rashtrapati Bhavan.

In 1952, and again in 1956, he was elected to the Rajya Sabha. He was not a very vocal member. When Dr Husain was India's delegate to UNESCO, Nehru offered him—and he accepted—the governorship of Bihar, and in 1962, the vice-presidentship of India.

In 1967, Mrs Gandhi backed him for the presidentship, which he won with a sizeable margin. He took no credit for this. 'My choice to this high office has mainly, if not entirely, been on account of my long association with the education of my people,' he said.

On one occasion, when I called on him in 1967, he spoke with concern about the growing division in the country. 'We are witnessing the atomization of our country. Our human material has not kept pace with our development.' The last time I saw him he spoke with sadness about the 'bad blood being created within the Cabinet' by the ambitious schemes of certain people.

An area about which he was deeply concerned was the North-East. He told me in 1968, 'If we offer one solution to the hill people of Assam, they won't take it, and if we offer another, the plains people won't accept it. What are we to do?' He heard, visibly moved, of how a leading hill leader, Stanley Nichols-Roy, had apologized to Assam's Chief Minister B.P. Chaliha for fomenting hatred. Soon after, when Dr Husain met Stanley Nichols-Roy, he said, 'If you can multiply this spirit among your colleagues, your state[*] can be the pioneer state of India.'

His last tour was to the North-East. It was there that he showed signs of exhaustion. He requested that his programme be cut down, but was persuaded to go through with it. On returning to Delhi, he died following a heart attack on 4 May 1969.

To those who had the privilege of knowing him, he was a warm friend. He gave his friendship selectively, but once given, he never took it back. When sitting with friends, he relaxed, tipped his white cap over his forehead, and spoke of what he really felt. In the presidential election campaign, some of his opponents spared no barb, a few communalists even questioned his loyalty to India. He was human enough to feel hurt, but too noble to hit back at them. He let his personality and work speak for itself.

By making him President, India honoured herself.

---

[*] Later to be formed and called Meghalaya.

Epilogue

Eminent Though Unknown

The preceding chapters are about eminent personalities who are well known, but there are several who, though unknown to the world, are eminent in their own way. My father was one of them. In the lives of each one of us—if one is fortunate—is one person who has taken a deep interest in one's growth and development either of character or of educational capabilities, or both. It may be a parent, a teacher or a friend, but they leave behind them a legacy deeply precious. To at least one other person that mentor is pre-eminent. In my case it was my father, Manekshaw P. Lala.

With his dark glasses, his balding forehead and his double-breasted suit, father looked a formidable figure to my childish eyes. A successful solicitor, he was at the peak of his career in my early childhood. But the awe he inspired vanished towards evening, when often, after a drive I would pretend to be asleep in the car so he would carry me up three flights of stairs.

He discouraged his clients from encroaching on his time at home and every night after supper he would devote to me. It was story time. He would inquire what my preference was for and relate a story or read a book to suit my mood. I must have rather worn him out asking for Sohrab and Rustom stories but he would always turn up with a fresh one. Thirty years later, when I asked where he had read them originally, he replied that he had made them up as he went along! *Aesop's Fables* and *Akbar and Birbal* were his favourites. When I was nine or so, he read me a book of proverbs and a fascinating book called *First Aid in English*. He would paint before my bewildered eyes the portrait of Falstaff or recite the story of Lancelot and Queen Guinevere, quoting a few verses from *Morte d' Arthur*.

William Wordsworth's grand-nephew was among those who had taught his generation English literature at Elphinstone College, Bombay. Father had an abiding love for literature and a remarkable memory which he kept alive by quoting his favourite lines, at times in season, and at other times, out of it! Short quotations like 'A thing of beauty is a joy forever' were frequent as he went through life, but extended quotations from Tennyson, Shelley and Keats were not infrequent. Occasionally, he would quote Firdausi in Persian which went over my head.

Father had a lighter side and if, for example, you mentioned Sir Walter Scott, you could be rest assured that he would come out with,

> Some fell by sabre, some by shot
> But none so flat as Sir Walter Scott.

As a child he got me fascinated with Dr Samuel Johnson 'drinking oceans of tea' and touching every alternate lamp-post as he ambled along the streets of London. Oliver Goldsmith—living in the garret to keep away his

Sketch by Mario Miranda

creditors—became an object of my childhood sympathy. When I was about twelve or thirteen he would sit beside me on the sofa on Saturday nights and read Macaulay's *Life of Johnson*. It proved such a hit that we went on to Macaulay's *Life of Goldsmith* and then of Addison.

Father probably enjoyed reliving his college days as much as I did. It was only decades later that I realized that the most precious thing father gave to me was—himself. He always had time for me.

But life was not all poetry. A tragedy had meanwhile struck our family. Mother left home. I was the only child, then ten years of age. It was decided that I would spend weekdays with mother and Saturdays and Sundays with father. The scar of the separation on me was somewhat healed as I was amply reassured of the affection of both my parents.

Mother was very modern for her times. In the 1930s hardly any of the ladies cropped their hair or drove a car in Bombay. She was a charming conversationist and, in her younger days, was accomplished in music and tailoring. During World War I, while in school, she had won a prize for the best oration at a major function in aid of soldiers and sailors at Bombay's grand Town Hall and counted it as the high point of her life.

Though there must have been many disagreements and arguments between father and mother, they were sensible and sensitive enough not to do so in my presence.

About the time of the separation I grew aware of the differences between my parents. Mother claimed that a friend of father's was diverting him from his legal practice and leading him astray on money matters.

This character, by promising my father a fortune in the

future, was liberally helping himself to father's current assets. After mother separated, father sold his car and shifted house. About a year after separation, on one Sunday morning father called me and said solemnly that he wanted to tell me something important. 'My son', he said, 'I am sorry. I won't be able to leave you any money. That man has deceived me.' He indicated that he had not only run through his wealth, but also what my late grandfather had intended for me.

It must have been a very difficult thing for him to say to a child. My heart went out to father, though I could say little. Decades later, I tried to fathom at what point of life I ceased to fear him. I think it was that moment of his honesty and need. He was no longer an awe-inspiring figure but as frail a human as I was. He became my friend because he was honest with me—his son.

His cheerful nature returned, though thereafter his legal practice never recouped. Money was just enough but never plentiful. There was one brief period of disagreement which we had but it soon passed.

We had some happy years together as I went through college and after. He used to tell me, 'I was never as free with my father as you are with me. I am more of a friend than a father.'

The separation and divorce and my mother remarrying another solicitor had cast a shadow over father and at times I could sense he was bitter. As he approached the age of eighty he relished saying brief prayers with me. After one such occasion, I ventured to ask him, for the first time, whether he was still bitter about mother. He turned to me and said, 'No son, not any more. It is no use being bitter.'

Some months after he had turned eighty, he fell seriously ill. For over two weeks he was in a coma, but he came out of it. The next days he could speak with difficulty, though he was audible. His senior physician said that even if he lived, he would live like a vegetable because a stroke had affected his brain. To test father's memory, one morning I read a verse from a poem I found quite difficult to remember—Shelley's *Indian Serenade*. That morning I asked father in hospital whether he remembered the lines,

> Oh lift me from the grass! I die! I faint! I fail!

In a moment he picked it up and with a tongue that dragged slowly, he recited,

> Let thy love and kisses rain
> On my lips and eyelids pale,
> My cheek is cold and white, alas!
> My heart beats loud and fast:-
> Oh! Press it close to thine again.
> Where it will break at last.

Five hours later, I got a phone call saying that he was no more.

When he departed, my father left no material possessions of consequence, but he left me treasures untold.

Select Bibliography

Chaliha, Jaya and Joly, Edward Le, *The Joy in Living—A Guide to Daily Living With Mother Teresa*, Penguin, 1997.

Dass, K.K., *Sucheta—An Unfinished Autobiography*, Navjivan Press, 1978.

Lala, R.M., *Beyond the Last Blue Mountain—A Life of J.R.D. Tata*, Penguin, 1995.

Lala, R.M., *The Joy of Achievement—Conversations with J.R.D. Tata*, Penguin, 1995.

Lala, R.M., *Celebration of the Cells*, Penguin, 1999.

Mankekar, D.R., *Lal Bahadur Shastri*, Builders of Modern India Series, Publication Division, Government of India, 1973.

Mukherjee, J.N., *Forward with Nature*, Popular Prakashan, 1979.

Swaminathan, M.S., *A Century of Hope*, East West Books, 1999.